COPING WITH

Homelessness

**Eugene Hurwitz
and Sue Hurwitz**

THE ROSEN PUBLISHING GROUP, INC./NEW YORK

Published in 1997 by The Rosen Publishing Group, Inc.
29 East 21st Street, New York, NY 10010

First Edition

Cover Photo by Kyle Wagner

Library of Congress Cataloging-in-Publication Data

Hurwitz, Eugene.
    Coping with Homelessness / Eugene Hurwitz and Sue Hurwitz.
      p. cm.
    Includes bibliographical references and index.
    Summary: Discusses the stresses with which homeless teens must
cope.
    ISBN 0-8239-2072-0
    1. Homeless Youth—United States—Social Conditions—Juvenile
literature. 2. Homelss youth—Services for—United States—Juvenile literature.   [1. Homeless persons.] I. Hurwitz, Sue, 1934-
II. Title.
HV4505.H86. 1997
305.235'086'942—dc21   97-17521
                                                         CIP
                                                         AC

ABOUT THE AUTHORS ◇

Eugene Hurwitz earned a B.S. in business at the University of Kansas and served four years in the United States Air Force. He worked as a commodity trader and taught seminars in market theory. He volunteers on a state health-insurance committee that supervises health benefits for at-risk recipients. He is the author of a visual trading method and the coauthor of *Working Together Against Homelessness*.

Sue Hurwitz earned an M.A. in education from the University of Missouri. She has taught every grade from preschool through ninth and has written twenty-three books, including *Working Together Against Homelessness* and *Coping With Deafness*.

TO JANIE
Thank you for the sunshine

Contents

Introduction

Are teens who run away from home considered homeless? Are families who move between relatives' houses regarded as homeless? What about people who sleep in their cars, in parks, or on public streets? How about people living in shelters? Are children living with relatives or in foster care counted among the homeless? All of these people may be viewed as homeless or at risk of homelessness.

Perhaps you or someone you know is living in such a situation. Perhaps when you hear about the homeless, you think it could never happen to you. But *anyone* can become homeless. A person is considered homeless if he or she lacks permanent housing and shelter or the ability to acquire and maintain a home of his or her own.

This book discusses homeless or near homeless teens on their own or with their families. You will read about some causes of homelessness and how some people cope with homelessness. You will read about people who became homeless due to circumstances beyond their control. You will read about other people who became homeless by choice. All teens should grow up with the security of knowing they will have all the basic needs of life fulfilled. All teens should have adequate food, shelter, health care, education, and other support systems. They should be given the opportunity to grow up and lead productive lives.

Unfortunately, many teens are homeless through no fault of their own. Many teens run away from abusive homes, are abandoned by their families and put into foster care, or are thrown out by their families. This book will give you some helpful resources if you find yourself living on the streets or find yourself at risk of becoming homeless. It will help you deal with many of the emotions you feel in this situation. It will also address ways in which you can use the community to help yourself and protect yourself against the dangers of life on the streets.

No matter where you live, you will find practical and healthy ways to deal with your situation. Teens living on the streets are found all over the country—in urban, suburban, and rural areas. They often find shelter in abandoned buildings or trailers, or in parks or other public places. Some teens turn to drugs or join gangs when they become homeless. Many think there is no way out of this situation.

To become homeless does not mean to become either *help*less or *hope*less. If you are concerned about a friend or yourself becoming homeless, remember that homelessness is often temporary. There are many organizations that exist to help the homeless: shelters, soup kitchens, mobile medical vans and drop-in clinics, services to treat sexually abused teens, and outreach programs that explore educational problems.

Being homeless is difficult for anyone, but it can be especially difficult for teens who are still learning how to take care of themselves. If you are a homeless teen, you may feel that no one understands what you're experiencing. But there are many organizations that exist to help you. Start with the resources mentioned in this book to help you get back into the mainstream of society.

Whether you find yourself at risk alone or with your family, you will most likely have to deal with many different feelings. Homelessness can make you feel embarrassed or ashamed, angry or powerless. These feelings are common. It's important to remember that recovery from homelessness or near homelessness takes time. But recovery *is* possible and it is achieved by many people every day.

CHAPTER 1

The History of Homelessness

The way society perceives the homeless has changed in recent years. In the past the word homeless was interchangeable with terms like bum, vagrant, and derelict. To be homeless was to be disconnected from society. The idea that homelessness simply means being without a permanent place to live or sleep is a recent phenomenon. In other words, the homeless people of today are quite different from the homeless of the past. Homelessness in the past was considered to be more a way of life than a condition resulting from circumstances beyond someone's control. Only in recent years has homelessness become a problem that society as whole recognizes the need to address and help.

Consider the following differences:

In the 1940s most homeless were able to work; most homeless people today are not considered employable by current standards.

Single women with children are the fastest-growing homeless population. The homeless population used to be made up of primarily white, single men.

The mentally ill were not permitted to roam the streets years ago. Today they are often found living on the streets.

In the past most immigrants were rapidly absorbed by society. President Theodore Roosevelt set up an adoption system for homeless immigrant children, which eventually placed one hundred thousand of them with families. Today, with the revised welfare system, many new immigrants will be denied assistance.

Twenty-five years ago the average age of a homeless person was fifty-seven. Today it is twenty-five.

During the 1800s the homeless received little sympathy or charity. More often than not, they lived in poorhouses where they were treated harshly and exploited as cheap labor. By the 1850s, settlement houses replaced poorhouses. They were funded by charities and donations from the rich, and they were more humane. Settlement houses provided job training, literacy classes and nurseries for children of working mothers.

Toward the end of the nineteenth century, transient workers—mainly men—moved about to find work. They lived in run-down, separate areas of cities called Skid Row. These areas often were located near railroad yards where men could hop on trains to move on. These homeless men were referred to as bums, hobos, tramps, or drifters. They received little sympathy or help from communities.

During the Great Depression of the 1930s, Americans faced the worst economic crisis in their history. Hundreds of thousands of workers lost their jobs. Large numbers of people adopted a migrant lifestyle, moving from place to place in search of work. This prompted the government to create many programs to help the poor.

Franklin D. Roosevelt first used the term "the New Deal" in 1932 when he accepted the Democratic party nomination for president. The New Deal was divided into two phases. The first phase occurred in 1933 and was created as a direct response to the Great Depression. The Great Depression was a result of the stock market crash of 1929. American society had never experienced such long and extreme poverty. At the height of the Depression, there were sixteen million unemployed people—one-third of the U.S. labor force. To give relief and recovery to the people suffering in the Great Depression, Congress created many emergency programs, such as the National Recovery Administration (NRA), the Agricultural Adjustment Administration (AAA), the Public Works Administration, and the Federal Deposit Insurance Corporation (FDIC).

In 1935 the Social Security system was established as the second phase, along with the National Youth Administration and the Wages and Hours Act. The Social Security Act provided people with unemployment insurance and old-age retirement insurance. It also provided federal grants to help states with programs for the elderly, the disabled, and needy children. That same year the Supreme Court struck down the NRA and AAA as being unconstitutional.

In 1937, the reforms of the New Deal came under attack from the Republican party. The Republicans felt there was too much money being spent on these programs and that taxes were too high as a result. Despite the criticism and opposition, many of the programs created under

Roosevelt's presidency remained intact until recently, most notably Aid to Families with Dependent Children (AFDC). They represented the core of American social policy.

In 1964, Lyndon B. Johnson, the thirty-sixth president, called for a nationwide war against poverty. This plan for economic and social welfare programs was designed to create what Johnson called the Great Society. Johnson's proposal rivaled the New Deal in its scope and push for government action to aid the poor.

Among the programs he created was a Medicare bill, which provided free medical care to the elderly collecting Social Security. A federal bill also was created to expand aid to education at all levels. Johnson also added a Department of Housing and Urban Development to the cabinet. These measures set out to provide tax reduction, an increased minimum wage, urban rehabilitation, and education reform.

In 1987, the United States Congress created the Stewart B. McKinney Homeless Assistance Act to address the growing needs of the country's homeless population. During that time, the homeless population was rapidly increasing and the issue was becoming more complex. Congress recognized that the problem was affecting a larger number of women and children than ever before. In response, Congress required states to ensure that all homeless children had the same rights to a free and appropriate education as nonhomeless children.

To help the states properly meet these new requirements, Congress gave money to the states to designate a coordinator for the education of homeless youth. The coordinator would gather data to obtain a better understanding of the challenges facing homeless youth. This collected data led Congress to amend the McKinney Act in 1990. The amended act was created to prohibit any barriers that prevented homeless youth from enrolling in school. The act was also intended to promote their academic success. The amendments were designed to research contributing factors that were keeping homeless youth out of school.

In 1994, the McKinney Act was amended yet again and included the Improving America's Schools Act. With these new amendments, the services were extended to include preschool children and the program worked to increase the legal protection of homeless youth.

In 1996, however, AFDC was eliminated by big changes in the welfare program. This meant there was no longer guaranteed assistance available to needy families and children. The reduction of AFDC greatly cut other welfare programs, such as food stamps and Social Security. It also greatly reduced the amount of benefits available to legal immigrants and their children. As part of the welfare changes, President Clinton and Congress passed the Personal Responsibility and Work Opportunity Reconciliation Act. This act replaced AFDC with Temporary Assistance for Needy Families (TANF). Under this program, the federal government provides block grants to states to assist poor families. The states have strict and important limits on the use of these block grants. The distribution of money is tightly tied to work, and there are strict time limits for receiving support.

Public Perceptions of Welfare

Welfare is an umbrella term for the variety of programs that provide income support and create a social safety net for impoverished individuals and families. Changes in welfare came at a time when the system fell under attack from many Americans. Organizations who work with the poor and the homeless believe that welfare recipients are misrepresented and that the new law is unfair. They believe that the current welfare reform is based on stereotypes and myths about welfare recipients and homeless people.

The myths about people on welfare are quite different from the reality. Many people believe welfare recipients are lazy and do not want to work. Women, in particular, are seen in an unflattering light. Some suggest that welfare mothers continue to have children in order to make money off the system. The facts, however, paint a very different picture.

Based on the annual benefits for a family on welfare, it seems unlikely that anyone is gaining financially. The combined benefits from AFDC and food stamps are, on average, about $8,700 for a family of three, which is at least 25 percent below the national poverty level. In addition, the average size of a family on welfare is smaller than the average American family. There are approximately 12.8 million people on welfare. Eight million of those are children. Since it is welfare assistance that is often the deciding factor in preventing homelessness, many believe the new, more restrictive act will force these children and their families onto the streets.

Without Social Security retirement benefits, almost half of Americans over the age of sixty-five would live in poverty. Even with Social Security, one out of every five older Americans lives near the poverty level or below, leaving many of them homeless or vulnerable to becoming homeless. About 55 percent of today's disabled homeless are eligible for Supplemental Security Income (SSI) benefits, but fewer than 30 percent are aware of or apply for SSI. Unfortunately, those who do receive SSI funds find them inadequate. And with the cuts from the welfare reform laws, the funds will be even less.

A 1996 study by the National Alliance to End Homelessness reports that approximately 750,000 Americans are without shelter on any given night. The study also estimates that 1.3 to 2 million Americans will be homeless at some point during the year. Another study estimates that by the year 2003, America could have nearly 19 million homeless people.

International Relief

Organizations such as the Red Cross, the World Health Organization (WHO), and the United Nations Children's Fund (UNICEF) were created to provide help to people throughout the world during times of crisis and in areas suffering from great poverty.

The Red Cross was started in 1863 as the brainchild of a Swiss citizen named Jean Henry Dunant, who urged relief for war victims. A Swiss welfare agency supported Dunant's suggestion. The next year, delegates from sixteen nations met in Switzerland and signed a proposal calling for the Amelioration (improvement) of the Condition of the Wounded and Sick of Armies in the Field. This protected medical personnel in time of war, and allowed them to treat wounded soldiers. It protected civilians who volunteered to help the organization. It also gave medical personnel and volunteers an international symbol to mark themselves and their supplies. The symbol honored Dunant by using the Swiss flag's colors in reverse—a red cross on a white background.

The American Red Cross was created in 1881 by Clara Barton. The organization is funded completely by voluntary contributions. The president of the United States is the honorary chairperson of the American Red Cross and is responsible for appointing its president and seven other board members. The American Red Cross provides relief for victims of natural disasters and sponsors special services for the armed forces and veterans, and public health and safety programs. Today there are over a hundred Red Cross organizations around the world.

The United Nations International Children's Emergency Fund (UNICEF) is an organization connected with the United Nations. It was created in 1946 to assist children and teens throughout the world, especially those in underdeveloped countries and countries devastated by war. UNICEF is also funded by voluntary contributions.

The problem of homelessness has existed for hundreds of years. The way society has perceived it and the way the government has responded to it have both changed dramatically. With the reforms of welfare under President Clinton's administration, many believe more people than ever before will be pushed into homelessness. This is clearly a time when the homeless and those at risk need to know what programs are available to help them. They also need to know how to cope and deal with their situations in order to work toward a new life.

CHAPTER 2

Who Are the Homeless?

People all over the world become homeless. Each person's or family's circumstances are unique, usually a combination of many factors. Because the homeless live in a constant state of transition, they are difficult to count. According to the American Homeless Society, however, studies estimate that 100 million people worldwide are completely homeless. About 1 billion people worldwide lack adequate housing.

GROUPS AMONG THE HOMELESS

Single Mothers and their Children

Women with children are among the fastest-growing homeless groups. They make up about 34 percent of the homeless population. The average homeless family consists of a single mother in her early twenties with two young children. Most likely, this mother does not have a high school diploma and cannot support her family. The reasons for homelessness among this group include poverty, abandonment, divorce, physical abuse, and single parenthood. It is estimated that the children of a homeless single mother are more likely to drop out of school and fall behind in their education than children who have permanent shelter. When these children grow up, some will continue the cycle of homelessness because of their educational disadvantages.

Teenagers

Teens are among the fastest growing homeless groups. According to the National Coalition for the Homeless, young people account for about 15 to 20 percent of the homeless population. These estimates do not include a large percentage of teens who are runaways or throwaways. Almost half of these young people have witnessed or experienced violence in their home. One of the most important problems facing homeless teens is education. The most recent Department of Education reports state that 18 percent of homeless students were not going to school. When a family becomes homeless, they often move around a lot, from shelters to relatives' or friends' houses to foster care families. This makes it difficult for teens to stay in school. Other obstacles include a lack of transportation, medical records and having no permanent address.

In 1987, the Education of Homeless Children and Youth Program was established by Congress. States are given money to develop programs to help homeless children stay and excel in public schools. The plan was extended in 1994 to include preschool children as well. With this program, the situation has improved, but many problems still remain. Homeless teens find it hard to stay motivated about school because they are dealing with major stress in their lives. Homeless teens are worrying about things such as food and shelter. School often takes a backseat to other basic needs. But getting an education is one of the most important things a homeless teen can do. School provides the skills to succeed throughout the rest of life.

Carla excelled in school. But her problems at home forced her to leave her home in Los Angeles when she was sixteen. Her father and brother had physically abused her since she was eleven. Her mother had died when she was ten. She felt she had no one to turn to for support. She decided to take her car and drive north to start a new life. She didn't anticipate that leaving home also meant sacrificing her education. She had dreams of going to college, but how would she ever get accepted without a high school diploma?

When Carla arrived in Portland, she entered a youth shelter and enrolled in the local public high school. But the people at the shelter told her they would have to take away her car if she wanted to continue living in the shelter. Carla didn't want to give up the car. It was her security blanket and it made her feel independent. It had gotten her out of an abusive situation and she was scared to be without it.

Carla began living in her car in the back of the school parking lot. But in order to stay in school Carla needed an address. Carla decided she wouldn't tell the school about her living arrangements. She wanted to stay in school and keep her car. The school thought she was still living in the youth shelter.

Living without a bathroom, a shower and a place to make food was very difficult and stressful. Carla would break into the school at night to wash herself and rummage through the school dumpsters for food. She felt very alone. She felt very different from her classmates. She couldn't confide in anyone and had trouble concentrating in class.

Carla couldn't get a part-time job without a permanent address, so she had to beg for money on the streets at night. When the weather got cold, Carla was forced to go back to the youth center. Again, the counselors told her she would have to sell her car. Carla was very upset. She couldn't continue living on the streets. It was too hard and her grades were starting to suffer. With some counseling, Carla decided that it was more important to get a good education. In the long run, it would be her schooling that would give her the independence she wanted and needed to succeed.

Veterans

About 135,000 to 400,00 veterans are homeless today. One out of every three homeless males has served in the U.S. armed forces. About 10 percent of veterans are homeless with families. Female veterans make up less than 2 percent of homeless veterans. About half of homeless veterans abuse alcohol or other drugs. Despite new efforts to reach homeless veterans, their legacy of physical problems, alcohol and substance abuse, unemployment, and homelessness continues to linger.

Alternative group housing where veterans can live under one roof appeals to some homeless veterans. This option helps them get off the streets. It also helps some of them to heal from the combat disability called post-traumatic stress disorder.

Austin was a veteran of the Gulf War. Austin hit rock bottom after his girlfriend kicked him out when she could no longer stand his addiction to alcohol. He had seen combat, disappointment in his parents' eyes, pity in his girlfriend's eyes, and distrust in the eyes of the general public. He was twenty-nine, but he felt at least twice that. Now he was homeless.

Austin pitched a tent in a wooded area that summer and managed to survive for three months. But by the end of October, the nights were too cold to sleep outdoors without protection. So Austin went into town and started sleeping at shelters.

The shelters made everyone leave at 6 AM and Austin had to fend for himself until the library opened at 10 o'clock. Day by day, he sat in the library and watched the clock. The minutes and his life struggled by at a snail's pace, and when Austin was sober, searching for ways to keep busy was intolerable.

One day, Austin attended a meeting at the shelter so that he could get out of the cold. He learned about Fresh Start, a sheltering program devoted to homeless veterans. He was sober enough at the time to want to get his life off hold and to try to heal himself. Fresh Start could help him do that.

Austin was required to attend Alcoholics Anonymous. He knew that it would be almost as difficult as facing combat, but he was determined to give it another try. With the help of other vets living through the same horror, maybe this time he could make it.

Austin, a former Marine, was intelligent and determined to beat his addictions. He attended counseling and AA meetings and learned that addiction is a disease. His self-esteem rose and he began to make progress in fighting his addictions.

Austin stayed at Fresh Start for almost two years, until he felt healed enough to venture out on his own. He enrolled in a community college using his G.I. Bill (government education benefits for veterans), and he is planning for a career as a drug counselor. He knew he could not have recovered without community help and he appreciated the services that assisted him.

As public awareness of the plight of veterans continues to grow, more and more local programs are providing alternatives for veterans.

People with Mental Illnesses

The mentally ill are the most visible people in the U.S. homeless population. About 23 percent of the homeless people whom we see living in public places have serious mental disorders. Evidence strongly suggests that deinstitutionalization has caused the high increase of homeless people.

While homeless families usually find temporary help in shelters and homeless teens are often placed in foster care or transitional housing, many mentally ill people stay on the streets. Mentally ill people are often homeless due to a lack of available treatment facilities. Without continual help, people who are mentally ill have a much harder time bringing their lives under control. Mentally ill people are often unable to access necessary treatment centers or find supportive housing services.

At the age of twelve, Quinton was institutionalized because of a mental disorder called schizophrenia. He had severe speech problems and was experiencing hallucinations. After years of therapy and the development of a new medicine, Quinton was able to get back in touch with reality. And, like tens of thousands of other institutionalized persons, he was released.

Quinton was now thirty years old. His father had died while he was hospitalized, but his mother was thrilled to have Quinton home and she tried hard to help him to care for himself. They got along pretty well for several months. But when Quinton's mother forgot to remind him to take his medicine every four hours, he suffered from mood swings and paranoid fantasies. During one of these episodes, Quinton ran away. His mother called the police but Quinton could not be found. Today Quinton is living on the streets. He is disoriented most of the time and does not know his name.

Unlike Quinton, many former residents of mental institutions do not have families or homes to go to when they are released. As a result, many mentally ill people are discharged and do not get the follow-up care they need to survive on their own. Without the tools to adapt to the outside world, they end up on the streets. These former patients need a more gradual reintroduction, so they are able to find food, shelter, and stay on their medication.

Physically Challenged Persons

In 1994, President Clinton addressed the problem of health care reform with access for all Americans. At that time, more than 37 million Americans had no health insurance. Without health insurance, chronic health problems often go untreated or receive less-than-adequate care. Such poor health often keeps people from working. Unless they have independent means, they are vulnerable to homelessness.

Although the physically challenged used to be considered disabled, many of these people are able to live independently. With medical treatment and accommodated housing, they can be rescued from homelessness. Government programs such as Social Security, Disability, or Supplemental Security payments financially assist the physically challenged. But these programs do not prevent some people from remaining vulnerable to homelessness.

Senior Citizens

The 1990 census revealed that about 12 percent of the U.S. population was sixty-five years old or older. This was approximately 31 million Americans. More than half had disabilities that limited their daily activities. By 1997, Medicare was financing health care for 38 million people who were elderly or disabled. Today the number of elderly and the number of people who are physically challenged continues to grow.

From 2.5 million to 4.9 million older Americans either go hungry or worry at times about their next meals. Some of these senior citizens become homeless. Many are in danger of becoming homeless. The Older Americans Act of 1965 established two major food programs. One program provides group meals to anyone over 60 and to their spouses regardless of age. These meals usually are served in senior centers or churches. The other program, Meals on Wheels, delivers food to people homebound with disabilities. To locate these programs, contact local agencies on aging, churches, health clinics, senior centers, and hospitals. More public awareness of the homeless and nearly–homeless elderly is slowly providing better accommodations to meet the needs of these senior citizens. Innovative day shelters that provide more than just a hot lunch are already established in some areas.

Refugees

Refugees are people who flee to another country to escape war, death, persecution, or a natural disaster. Refugees are the largest group of homeless people worldwide. Their number has escalated during the last two decades to reach 23 million. According to a recent report by the United Nations High Commissioner for Refugees (UNHCR), one out of every 114 people in the world have been uprooted by conflict. Many of today's refugees come from Rwanda, Afghanistan, Cambodia, Ethiopia, Nicaragua, and the former Yugoslavia. Other refugees are displaced from Somalia, Angola, the former Soviet Union, and Vietnam.

Enti and his family are one example of refugees. Enti, his wife, his son Cyu, and his two daughters lived in Rwanda. In April, 1994, the Rwandan president, a member of the Hutu tribe, was killed in a plane crash. The Hutu charged that the other major ethnic group in Rwanda, the Tutsi, were responsible. The Hutu army began burning Tutsi homes and slaughtering every Tutsi in sight. Enti and his family barely escaped the machetes of the Hutu army. They were sheltered for a while by a sympathetic Hutu family in the hills. But soon, even such Hutus were no longer safe.

When the Hutu army stormed their village, Enti's family became scattered. Although Enti and his son later searched for his wife and daughters, they never found them.

The United Nations provided refuge for Enti and Cyu, and arranged for them to leave Rwanda. They flew on a Belgian plane to an International Red Cross refugee camp in Nairobi, Kenya. While they waited for relocation, Enti learned that more than a million Rwandan refugees had fled to neighboring Zaire. At the camps in Zaire, a cholera epidemic killed many hundreds of victims each day.

With assistance from the United States, the epidemic was brought under control in several weeks. The Zairean government urged the refugees to return to Rwanda. They claimed the Hutu had fled after their four-month slaughter of the Tutsi, and assured the Tutsi that they would be safe in Rwanda now. When Enti and Cyu boarded a plane from Nairobi to the United States, Enti was consumed with grief and prayed constantly.

Enti and Cyu found temporary housing in the United States at a community center affiliated with the Immigration and Refugee Services of America. Social workers at the center discovered that Enti spoke French as well as Swahili. Through a French interpreter they learned that he had been a carpenter. Enti and Cyu were placed in short-term housing with a Cuban refugee family. They both received counseling at the community center. But what could help someone who had lost his family and had seen friends butchered right before his eyes? What could help a six-year-old child who was abruptly torn away from his mother and sisters? The counselors believed that Enti and Cyu would cope better with their losses if they kept busy. The center tried to find Enti a job as a carpenter. Enti wanted to bring his family to America if they were found, so they could start a new life together. Enti hoped that one day soon his prayers would be answered.

Illegal Immigrants

Unlike refugees who are displaced from their homes by war, ethnic persecution, or natural disasters, immigrants choose to leave their native countries. Their reasons for leaving may include a desire for better economic opportunities, for political freedom, or for the chance to start over in a new country.

According to a recent report by the Immigration and Naturalization Service (INS), more than three-fifths of all illegal residents in the United States come from Central America and the Caribbean. About one-third come from Mexico. Others come from Canada, Europe, Asia, South America, and Africa.

The term "illegal immigrant" or "illegal alien" means that the person either entered the United States without getting the documentation required by the U.S. government, or entered with legal documentation to visit or study but did not leave the United States when the stay ended. More than 4 million illegal immigrants presently live in the United States. It is estimated that 300,000 more enter and settle here each year.

The INS gears most of its efforts toward stopping people from illegally crossing U.S. borders. Yet more than 50 percent of the illegal population enters legally as tourists, students, or temporary workers. When their visas expire, they simply do not leave. National welfare reform that became law in 1996 now denies most welfare benefits to illegal immigrants, and to legal immigrants who are not United States citizens and their children. This legislation allows each state to decide whether to continue providing medical care to elderly noncitizens.

With little knowledge of English, illegal immigrants cannot find jobs that pay enough for them to live on. To avoid detection, they may move constantly, often living on the streets or in inadequate make–shift housing without water or electricity. Many illegals become homeless. Even more constantly live at risk of becoming homeless. The fate of immigrants who enter the United States legally and then fail to leave is usually better than those immigrants who enter illegally. Tourists, students, or executives of international companies often have some knowledge of English and may come from a privileged background. Many of these people open restaurants or other independent businesses and have a better life than they left back home.

Migrant Workers

There are 3 to 5 million migrant and seasonal farm workers throughout the United States. Most of these people have legal status, but some are in the country illegally from Mexico, other Latin American countries, or the Caribbean countries. Because of their transient, crowded lifestyles and poor working and living conditions, migrant workers are vulnerable to many health problems. Heat stress, toxic chemicals in pesticides, and parasitic infections from contaminated water are constant work hazards. Although federal money for migrant health care has long been available, many states show little interest in applying for these funds. The Public Health Service budgets close to $60 million for migrant health care nationwide. But its services reach only about 500,000 workers.

Today, the American homeless have rights to federal and state government services that have been established to help them. But the services are changing and becoming more complex. The homeless must learn how to get these benefits and how to use them. The homeless must be encouraged to get help, and to find solutions to the problems that caused their homelessness. The nearly homeless and others who are vulnerable must be encouraged to actively search for ways to avoid becoming homeless.

Homelessness is often the cause, not the result, of many physical and mental disorders. Alcoholism and substance abuse frequently develop or get worse after people become homeless. In this chapter you have read about some of the many faces of homelessness. If you have friends or relatives who need help, encourage them to seek out the social agencies that can help them. As you can see, there is no glamour or freedom in being homeless and living on the streets. Homelessness is an extremely stressful and painful condition.

CHAPTER 3

How Does Homelessness Happen?

Homelessness happens when people can no longer take responsibility for themselves. They have exhausted the usual networks of support—family, friends, neighbors—and they simply cannot cope any longer. The problems that contribute to homelessness usually begin long before a person or family actually has no home. Unemployment or underemployment with an inadequate income lead to prolonged poverty. A fixed income with rising housing expenses leaves many people vulnerable to homelessness. A lack of educational opportunity frequently leads to homelessness. Personal crises such as job loss, health problems, domestic problems, substance abuse, or natural disasters push vulnerable people into homelessness.

Nearly one-fourth of the world's population, 1.2 billion people, lives in poverty. Poverty makes people extremely vulnerable to homelessness. On any given day, 40,000 homeless people roam the streets of London. About 1,000 children die of malnutrition every month on the streets of Haiti. In some countries, the population greatly exceeds the housing resources. The extremely poor rarely have an opportunity to better their situation for themselves or their families.

Myths About the Homeless

You may have certain ideas about how people become homeless. Homeless people suffer from much prejudice. Many people make unfair judgments about the homeless in order to ignore them and the problems they face.

The most common myths about homeless people are as follows:

- *Most homeless people are mentally ill.*

The mentally ill make up about 23 percent of the homeless population. Studies have shown that the form of illness many of them suffer from is depression. Studies also show that homelessness is the cause, not the result, of this depression. Many of the homeless who are now mentally ill did not have any psychological problems before they became homeless. Therefore, it is clear that mental illness is not the main contribution to homelessness.

- *Most homeless people abuse drugs and alcohol.*

Substance abusers make up about 33 percent of the homeless population. Unfortunately, many substance abusers who are poor do not have the money to get proper treatment. There is unfair prejudice against poor drug abusers in our society. Many drug abusers who can afford to get help do not suffer the same consequences of their actions, nor do they suffer the same stigma as the poorer drug abusers. It is also common for drug and alcohol abuse to occur as the result of homelessness.

- *Most homeless people are lazy and do not want to work.*

The truth is that most of the homeless population wants to work but they lack the education, a permanent address (most jobs require you to fill out an application with your home address and telephone number), and the proper skills. Homeless people also frequently lack the self-confidence necessary to apply for a good job.

In most places in the United States, 30 percent of the homeless are working. They just don't earn enough money for food and housing for themselves or their families.

REASONS FOR HOMELESSNESS

Poverty

America is one of the wealthiest countries in the world, yet poverty is a very real problem for millions of people. Poverty is the major cause of hunger and of homelessness. From 1970 to 1995, the number of poor people in the United States increased from 25.4 million to 31.9 million. Of these, 40 percent are children. The rise in poverty is due to two major factors. One is the lack of job opportunities, the other is the recent decrease in public assistance.

One of the contributing causes to fewer work opportunities is the fact that wages have declined. Between 1973 and 1993, the percentage of workers earning wages below the poverty line increased from 23.9 percent to 26.9 percent. Declining wages have made it extremely difficult for many workers to afford housing. In most states, families must earn at least double the minimum wage to afford decent housing.

A lack of affordable housing has forced many families into homelessness and put even more at risk. While 2.2 million low-rent housing units disappeared in the last twenty years, the number of people in need of low-rent housing increased from 7.4 million to 11.2 million. A study from the U.S. Department of Housing and Urban Development found that the majority of people with housing needs were families with children, elderly people, and disabled individuals. These groups of people, as was stated earlier, become especially vulnerable to homelessness.

Homelessness and poverty are inherently linked. Those who are poor have trouble paying for housing, food, health care, and education. When families have limited resources, sacrifices must be made. Since housing is the most expensive element, it is most often dropped in times of need. People with limited job skills and limited income often become homeless for short periods of time. The loss of a job or a medical crisis makes their housing suddenly unaffordable. Many people are just one paycheck away from homelessness. They may live temporarily with relatives or in shelters until their crisis passes and they are able to save money. Temporary homelessness does not have as drastic a result on a person's life as does chronic homelessness.

Single Parenthood

Many homeless people are single parents. Homeless single mothers usually have weak supportive relationships and few options. It is very difficult to work and raise children. Many single parents cannot afford to pay for day care for their children and few companies provide daycare facilities for their employees. If there is no one to care for the children, the parent cannot work. In many cases substance abuse or illness makes working impossible and leaves them homeless or nearly homeless.

Adam's family became homeless after a slow descent into poverty. Adam and his sister Molly lived a comfortable life until his father abandoned the family when he was in third grade. Although Adam's mother held a steady job as a receptionist, she could not earn enough money to pay all their bills. With only one paycheck, the family had to alter their lifestyle drastically. They were forced to move into a tiny apartment. They had to begin shopping at thrift stores. Adam accepted his cousin's used clothing, but he felt embarrassed because the shirts and trousers never fit him very well.

Adam's mother, who was chronically depressed, became a heavy drinker. She neglected her appearance and she could not handle her job efficiently. Every time Adam's mother got fired from a job, she began drinking even more. By the end of that school year, Adam's mother left the apartment only to buy more liquor. Life became more and more unbearable for Adam and Molly. Their mother slept a lot, but when she was awake she spent most of the time yelling or crying. She often got angry and hit Molly for no apparent reason. She ranted on and on about her absent, no-good husband.

Conditions at home deteriorated steadily. The gas and the electricity were often turned off for several days until their Aunt Claire paid the bills. They also had little to eat. Adam felt humiliated by his family's lack of money and he became preoccupied with hiding their problems. Even though Adam did not tell anyone about the dreadful conditions at home, he suspected that everyone knew. Adam avoided his peers at school because he felt different from them. He felt alienated and became withdrawn.

When Adam entered junior high, he finally confided in his school counselor, who helped him apply for the school lunch program for himself and Molly. The school counselor put Adam in touch with other resource people. He also helped Adam find a part-time job after school tutoring and baby-sitting. Though the job did not pay much money, working helped enormously in improving Adam's outlook. But the final blow came when they got an eviction notice because they had not paid rent for nearly a year. Adam and his family became homeless due to poverty.

Aunt Claire would not take them in for more than a few nights. Because of Adam's mother's drinking problem, his aunt did not want his mother around her four children for long. They stored a few things at Aunt Claire's apartment and Adam, Molly, and their mother moved to a shelter. When Adam's mother was interviewed at the shelter she was urged to go to a mental health clinic and enter a program for alcoholics. She was so sick and tired that she did not fight it.

Adam and Molly moved back to their aunt's apartment while their mother received treatment. After their mother completed her therapy, she applied for welfare assistance and several days later they all moved to another shelter. After several months, Adam's mother found a job. She attended Alcoholics Anonymous meetings on a regular basis to help her stay sober. With monthly checks from Temporary Assistance for Needy Families (TANF), the family was able to move into their own apartment. In time they were able to bring their lives under control.

Adam's mother was one of the numerous working poor who simply could not earn enough money to support her family with one paycheck. After Adam's father abandoned the family and stopped providing financial support, a decline in their standard of living was inevitable. By seeking the help of his school counselor, Adam learned about available options to help his family recover. Without the help of government and community programs, the family may never have been able to break the cycle of poverty.

Adam was wise to talk with his school counselor about his problems when he could no longer cope on his own. But he might have prevented a lot of suffering if he had looked for help earlier. When his family could no longer survive on their own, Adam should have looked to the community for help. Adam could have checked with a Salvation Army soup kitchen to help ease their hunger. He could have asked a social service agency, the American Red Cross, or a church to help the family. But after the family learned how to find community agencies to help them, they were able to cope better with their homelessness.

Substance Abuse

While many who are addicted to alcohol and drugs are not homeless, people who are poor and suffering from chemical dependence put themselves at risk of homelessness. Abusing drugs does increase the risk for those who are already one step away from losing their housing.

Unfortunately, those who do end up on the streets because of substance abuse have a difficult time getting their lives under control. Some take the first step of getting treatment, only to find that successful graduates of treatment programs are discharged and back onto the street, increasing the chances of relapse. A 1992 study of service providers reported that 80 percent of local treatment centers could not meet the demand of homeless substance abusers and had to turn them away.

Unfortunately, new policy changes will deny benefits to substance abusers whose chemical dependence has contributed to their homelessness. Without proper treatment, homeless addicts have great difficulty recovering from their situation. Even when they do succeed in getting treatment for the disease, the lack of assistance causes a great chance of relapse.

Domestic Violence

Domestic violence occurs among all races and socioeconomic groups and is likely to occur at least once in two-thirds of all marriages. National Crime Survey data shows that approximately one-third of women victimized by domestic violence will be victimized again during the following six months. Women receiving shelter services usually report frequent and severe abuse. Battered women who live in poverty are often forced to choose between homelessness and an abusive relationship.

Studies estimate that 3 to 4 million American women are battered each year by their husbands or partners. These figures do not account for the many thousands of cases of domestic violence that go unreported. Each year more than 1 million women need medical assistance for injuries caused by battering. Research suggests that around 30 percent of battered women are pregnant at the time. These women have nearly twice as many miscar- riages as nonbattered women. Some data suggests that wife-beating results in severe injuries requiring medical treatment more often than rape, auto accidents, and mug- gings combined.

According to a Bureau of Justice Statistics report, about 95 percent of the victims of domestic violence are women. Other recent studies suggest that men experience physi- cal abuse almost as often as women. Perhaps male victims of domestic violence are now reporting abuse more fre- quently, or perhaps female victims are still underreport- ing such abuse. Since domestic violence takes place in the home, it is difficult to gather information unless the vio- lence is reported to authorities.

A study of homeless women conducted by the Better Homes Fund reported that 91 percent of the mothers had experienced physical or sexual abuse at some point in their lives. If you or someone you know is in an abusive relationship or is about to become a runaway or throw- away because of violence at home, think about the hazards of living on the streets. The streets are a high-risk envi- ronment. Call one or more of the crisis hot lines or agen- cies listed at the back of this book. Let them help you cope with your situation before you face homelessness on your own. Perhaps you have more alternatives than you realize. If you already are homeless and have not con- tacted these hot lines or agencies, do so at once. Let the community help you.

Lack of Education

School-age children living in shelters exhibit high levels of anxiety and depression. They frequently suffer from emotional and learning problems if they stay in shelters for a long period of time. Preschoolers have an even harder time. They may develop problems with their speech and motor skills. Homeless children who do attend school face many obstacles and endure many difficulties. They are often concerned that the other students will find out that they are homeless. They may feel ashamed and embarrassed by their situation.

They may be distracted by the crises going on within their families and may be unable to concentrate on their studies. They may not have proper clothing and supplies or an adequate place to do their homework. Sometimes they cannot even figure out how to get to a school. Even when it is temporary, this lack of opportunity can negatively affect their future. Without a proper education, it becomes even more difficult to break the cycle of poverty in which they grew up.

Joel was eleven when his father and mother divorced. Joel and his mother moved in with his grandmother, making a total of nine relatives living in one apartment. Life was difficult in such a crowded environment. There were constant fights, and the apartment was always filled with tension for one reason or another. Joel found the lack of privacy very stressful.

"I can't do anything, Mom," he complained. "I'm not allowed to watch the TV programs I want, I can't play music. Grandma's apartment is so noisy that I can't even hear myself think!"

Finally his mother decided that they had to leave. She and Joel moved to a nearby shelter but it was dirty and had rats and roaches. Still, a social worker at the shelter helped Joel's mother apply for welfare benefits. She also found her a job on the staff of a large hotel. After several nights, Joel and his mother transferred to a "transitional facility" for homeless families run by the American Red Cross. This shelter was clean. No rats, no roaches. They had a room with a TV and a clean shower and bathroom just down the hall.

There were other children in this shelter and a school bus stopped by each day to take them to school. The social worker placed their name on a list for federally assisted housing. Joel studied hard at school and was an excellent student. He helped tutor younger children at the shelter and discovered that he enjoyed doing it. He hoped to earn a college scholarship later to help him get a degree in education. Their social worker told Joel that funding programs were available for high-school students with ability and need.

Natural Disasters

Natural disasters such as floods, earthquakes, droughts, hurricanes, or tornadoes occur all over the world. Such disasters often suddenly wipe out people's homes and life savings. Many are plunged into immediate homelessness from which they never recover. Today, 1.2 million trained American Red Cross volunteers are dedicated to helping their neighbors across the country recover from natural disasters. American Red Cross volunteers are at the scene of more than 40,000 disasters a year, from fires and floods to hurricanes and tornadoes.

Zoe and her family were forced out of their home by flood. After four days of steady rain, the Mississippi River overflowed its banks. High water spread over levees and cornfields. Sirens sounded, warning people to hurry to high ground. Zoe packed as many possessions as possible into their car. She and her two children and her mother abandoned their mobile home for an emergency shelter quickly set up in the town school.

Zoe didn't sleep a wink that night. She tossed and turned with worry. A steady rain pounded against the windows. The next morning, while standing on a bluff overlooking the sea of floodwater, Zoe and her mom saw their home sitting in waist-high water. They returned to the shelter in a state of shock. Depression and tears soon followed. Both Zoe and her mom could barely cope. They had no insurance and no savings. Everything they owned probably had been destroyed or ruined. What could they do? Where would they live? How could Zoe care for her children?

After another sleepless night, Zoe and her mom began to consider their future. They applied for public assistance as suggested by a relief worker. Meanwhile, the American Red Cross gave them food and clothing vouchers. The Red Cross also issued lodging vouchers so they could stay in a motel until they received their welfare check. Zoe and her mom appreciated the disaster emergency help. But it was only a band-aid measure. They still needed a place to sleep and an income to supplement the welfare money. Zoe had donated time at a local church's preschool so that her children could attend for free. She asked her minister for advice. By the end of the following day, Zoe had been offered the use of the church's old school bus for shelter.

Zoe and her mom were delighted to hear this, especially after they entered their old trailer and found layers of mud covering their possessions. Using some of the money given to them by the Red Cross, they bought a kerosene lantern and a chemical toilet. Their new living quarters did not provide much room, but they were grateful to have a roof over their heads.

At age thirty-six, Zoe had been the victim of domestic violence and had been homeless once before. Now, as the victim of a flood, she was homeless again. Her former husband beat her and abused drugs. She'd had no choice but to leave him. Zoe had been vulnerable to homelessness since the night she ran away to a women's shelter. Yet she considered herself lucky that she was free from physical abuse. The women at the shelter had given her immediate refuge. After she contacted her mother in another town, they gave Zoe and her children money to travel to her mother's home.

In addition to collecting welfare and food stamps, Zoe learned about a job-training program offered through the welfare agency. She welcomed an opportunity to learn a job skill that would enable her to support herself and her kids. Although Zoe and her family were victims of one of the tens of thousands of natural disasters that occur each year, she was resourceful enough not to remain homeless for long. With emergency help from the American Red Cross and temporary help through the charity of her church, Zoe and her family soon were able to move from the shelter. Additional government help and job training make Zoe's prospects for escaping her homelessness look promising.

Zoe used the temporary help from community agencies to pull her life together. By benefiting from job training, Zoe should be able to become self-sufficient and live a normal life again. Emergency services provided by the Red Cross include food, clothing, temporary housing, household furnishings, linens, bedding, medical needs, and emergency minor home repairs. Volunteers also teach a variety of safety and health skills such as Cardiopulmonary Resuscitation (CPR), first aid, water safety, and health courses. They collect and distribute about 6 million units of blood yearly in local blood drives to help disaster victims worldwide. Americans suffering from a natural disaster may also be eligible for federal funds if their town has been declared a disaster area by federal officials. The American Red Cross is a leading provider of disaster and emergency services. All Red Cross disaster assistance is free. The Red Cross receives no government funding. The organization relies on private donations.

The U.S. Federal Emergency Management Agency (FEMA) has published a checklist to help minimize the effects of any natural disaster. This list is a disaster supplies checklist and may make your situation a bit easier to handle.

— At least three gallons of bottled water per person (one per day) in sealed plastic containers (several times this amount of water should be stored for floods, hurricanes, and blizzards)
— Canned foods: fruits, vegetables, meat, milk (or milk powder), beans, etc. that do not need cooking
— Sealed or packaged foods that do not need refrigeration, such as granola bars, cookies, and dried fruit—altogether, enough food for two weeks
— A hand-operated can opener and bottle openers
— Flashlights and battery-operated radio with extra batteries (A battery-powered weather radio that receives only continuous weather reports is sold in electronics stores for about $20)
— Candles and matches (protected against moisture)
— A heat source (camp stove or canned heat)—use with care!
— Blankets and sleeping bags

— Rain gear and extra clothing, including sturdy shoes and (in cold conditions) warm outerwear
— Credit cards and extra cash
— A complete first-aid kit (buy the best)
— A list of medications, doctors' telephone numbers, and other medically related family information
— Extra car keys
— Spare eyeglasses (if you or your family members wear them)
— Toilet paper, paper towels, plastic trash/garbage bags
— Valuables (personal papers, jewelry, etc.)

This is only the most basic list for any disaster emergency. Your supplies should be kept together, in an accessible place. Every member of the family should know where these supplies are kept. If possible, take them with you if you must leave home in a disaster emergency.

It's clear that there are many different factors that can contribute to homelessness. The circumstances are complex, and they force people to make hard choices about food, shelter, and education. In Adam's case, he and his family slowly progressed into homelessness as their situation got worse and worse. In Zoe's case, however, homelessness was unexpected and sudden. Either way, becoming homeless is a major upheaval in your life. Getting the help you need to recover from the situation is vital. In the next two chapters, we'll specifically discuss homeless teens who are living on the streets alone and the issues they must face.

CHAPTER 4

Homeless Teens

recent study by the U.S. Department of Health and Human Services divided youths on the streets into three categories:

1. Homeless youths—those who spend one or more nights in a shelter, a public place, an abandoned building, a car or subway, or outside. These youths may be with or without their families.
2. Runaway youths—those who spend one or more nights away from home without permission from parents or guardians. This category also includes youths who may have left home or an institution with permission but who did not return as expected.
3. Throwaway youths—those who spend one or more nights away from home when their parent or guardian knew they were leaving but did not care. This includes youths who were told to leave home.

Some teens engage in a risky lifestyle complicated by drug or alcohol abuse, teenage parenthood, or sexually

transmitted diseases. One-fourth of all adolescents contract a sexually transmitted disease before graduation
from high school. These behaviors are on the rise and
often contribute to teens' homelessness. Some teen counseling programs advise youths at risk to use survival skills
to help them avoid trouble. Many programs recommend
the following:

1. Don't take dares.
2. Don't act tough.
3. Walk away from trouble.
4. Love and respect your parents.
5. Learn in school.
6. Join team sports to channel pent-up energy.
7. Enjoy being a teen, don't try to grow up fast.

CAUSES OF TEEN HOMELESSNESS

Teenage Pregnancy

A study from Advocates for Youth shows that 2,800 teens
will give birth each day. Less than 5 percent of these
teenagers choose to deliver their babies and put them up
for adoption. Approximately 44 percent choose to keep
their babies. Although 37 percent of pregnant teens
choose to abort their pregnancy, more than 500,000
babies are born each year to teenage mothers. For many
young mothers, there is no place to turn. Many teens are
forced to leave home because their parents don't want a
baby around or can't support them.

Private and publicly funded group homes and care
centers are available in some communities and cities for
young pregnant women who can no longer stay at home.
These places offer pregnant teens and teen mothers a

place to live and receive child care, financial support, and counseling, while they complete their education and get job training. One such program is run by Homes for the Homeless (HFH). Since 1986, the organization has helped over eight thousand families and over eighteen thousand children. HFH runs four American Family Inns, and the residents must follows strict rules and regulations, including:

- All residents must be in by 10:30 PM.
- No men are allowed past the visitor's lounge.
- No alcohol or drugs allowed.

If any rules are broken, privileges are taken away. A resident can be kicked out permanently for bad behavior.

The young women are provided with an apartment for one year and a large variety of services that give teen mothers a chance to improve their lives. They can take high-school courses, learn about child care, and get job training and housing advice. No one is required to take part in any activity, but positive peer pressure usually encourages participation. Many of these kinds of houses report that high percentages of the young women get their high school diplomas. There are many houses like the ones run by HFH around the United States. Many are small and privately run. If you find yourself pregnant and are worried about ending up on the streets, contact one of the organizations at the end of this book to find a local teen-parent residence.

For teen mothers, the new restrictions in public policy require them to live with a parent or adult guardian in order to receive welfare benefits. The ACLU believes this is a violation of civil liberties. According to the U.S. Department of Health and Human Services, 66 percent of teen mothers reported that they had been sexually abused. Fifty-four percent of those reported being molested by a family member.

Teen pregnancy has shown a slight decline since 1994. The decline probably is due to increased abstinence, more condom use, and a growing fear of disease and HIV infection among high school students. Yet abstinence is the only sure way to avoid pregnancy.

Brandy became pregnant when she was fifteen years old. The baby's father abandoned her and the baby when the responsibilities became too great. Brandy was living with her mother for a while, but soon left home because of her mother's drug addiction. Brandy was scared about leaving, but her mother's heroin addiction was interfering with caring for her baby. Brandy loved her son and wanted to give him a good home. She also wanted to give herself a better future.

Through a counselor at school, she found out about a place where she could live and enroll in a program that would let her take classes and care for her baby. Sometimes she just wants to go off with her friends and she doesn't feel like following all the rules. But she knows that her son is depending on her. Brandy is up early every day. She drops off her baby at day-care and goes to work. Brandy gets job training in the morning and attends class in the afternoon. It's a long and hard schedule, and she is often tired by the end of the day. But in six months, Brandy will graduate and hopefully become self-sufficient. She feels bad that her son will grow up without his father, but she's happy she's not on the streets.

Running Away

More than 1 million American children and youths become homeless each year. Some studies estimate that approximately 10 percent of today's homeless are teen runaways. The number of runaways fleeing from physical, mental, or sexual abuse at home is declining. Still, as many as 70 percent of runaways were physically or sexually abused in their homes. Once homeless, nearly 90 percent of minors engage in prostitution or pornography in order to survive. This number includes teens who have not been physically or mentally abused but who still choose to run away from home.

Vanessa was a preschooler when her brother began sexually abusing her. She did not know that sexually abusing a family member was called incest. All she knew was that Sam punched her, slapped her, and hurt her. After Vanessa started elementary school she began to scream at Sam to stop. She would run and hide in her room when her father and stepmother left the house. But Sam always found her and molested her. He threatened to kill her if she told anyone, and Vanessa believed him.

Vanessa begged her parents not to leave her home alone with Sam, but they never paid attention. They never noticed the bruises on Vanessa. They always told Vanessa to stop behaving like a baby. By the time Vanessa was eleven, she had constant pains in her stomach and could not eat. She could not concentrate on her schoolwork. One evening when her parents went out to dinner, she ran away while Sam was talking on the telephone.

When it began to get dark, she became terrified and went to a nearby mall. A woman saw her alone and crying. She sat down next to Vanessa and began talking to her. After discovering that she was a runaway, the woman told Vanessa that she was beautiful and said that she could get Vanessa a job as a photo model. She said that her name was Glenda and offered to introduce Vanessa to her boyfriend who was going to pick her up soon.

The woman bought Vanessa dinner. When her boyfriend arrived, he seemed nice and friendly. Vanessa was impressed with his shiny red car. So she left the mall with Glenda. Vanessa had run away from home because of sexual abuse, and ended up in a life of pornography and prostitution. She was hustled out of town, and although she was treated kindly, she was never given any money. Glenda kept a twenty-four-hour watch over Vanessa so she could not run away.

Glenda and her boyfriend were constantly on the road, moving from city to city. At first Vanessa enjoyed the excitement and attention. They asked her to pose nude while they photographed her. She did not mind posing nude after the first few times. But Glenda began bringing in more and more "friends" for Vanessa to "entertain" sexually. Vanessa began to feel used and dirty. She realized she was no better off now than she had been at home; her body was still being violated.

One day when they stopped in a truck stop to eat, Vanessa went to the rest room. There she saw a runaway hot line telephone number taped to the mirror. Although she trembled with fear, Vanessa copied down the number. Several days later, Vanessa slipped away from Glenda's watchful eye and called the runaway hot line. She was directed to a temporary shelter, counseling, and foster care.

Eventually, with counseling, Vanessa felt strong enough to confront her parents and she called home. When Vanessa's parents came to meet with Vanessa, they were aloof and the meeting was awkward. Vanessa's social worker recommended counseling for Vanessa's parents. But they refused to admit that they were at fault for anything that happened to Vanessa. Vanessa refused to return to her parents' house even though they reluctantly offered to take her home. She chose to stay in foster care and continue with her schooling. She hoped that some day she might be able to feel like a whole person again.

Although it was difficult, Vanessa made a wise decision when she chose not to return to her parents' home. With counseling and schooling she was learning to deal with her former abuse. She knew it would take time and effort on her part before she got better. But she wanted to start a new life and she probably could not have done that if she had returned home. Her parents were reluctant to admit the family had problems and most likely would have refused to participate in any therapy.

Throwaways

Today's homeless children and teens are more troubled than in previous years and the overall numbers are increasing. "Throwaways" and "system kids" who run away from foster care or institutions account for half of the youths generally thought of as runaways. According to Advocates for Youth, one-quarter of all gay males choose to leave or is forced out of their homes because of their sexual orientation.

At sixteen, Jay left home when he tested positive for HIV. When Jay told his parents, they were very upset. His father was stoic; his sisters were stunned. Only his mother cried. "Go back to your friends," Jay's father finally shouted. "They can watch you die. We want no part of it!"

"I have nowhere else to go," Jay said.

"I don't want your younger sisters to live with this shame," Jay's father continued. "We don't want our friends to know you have AIDS."

Jay felt devastated by his family's lack of compassion. He was growing more ill every day. He longed for the comfort and care that he'd hoped they would offer him. Most of all, he yearned for them to understand his mental anguish. But they didn't. Reluctantly, Jay accepted money and headed north to San Francisco. He spent months living on the street and in shelters.

Jay couldn't believe that his family was so cold and prejudiced. He'd told them he was too sick to work now and couldn't take care of himself. He hadn't even finished high school. But they were not willing to take care of him. How did they think he would survive? When Jay began to get sick, he looked to the community for help. A case worker found him an opening in a twenty-four-unit residence recently built for single men and women and youths suffering from AIDS. She sent Jay to a clinic to assess his physical condition and medication. Then Jay could transfer to the residence house for as long as necessary. Jay was fortunate to receive medical treatment and find shelter. Without community support, he would have been on the streets with nowhere to turn. Jay learned to cope with homelessness.

The Department of Housing and Urban Development (HUD) provides federal grants to nonprofit organizations to build residences for AIDS victims. HUD also provides funds for rental assistance to single, poor AIDS victims, and needy AIDS families. Many times the locations of these residences are kept confidential to maintain the privacy and security of the people living there. Unfortunately, some citizens would complain if they knew that residences for homeless people or AIDS victims were created in their neighborhoods.

Teens Choosing Homelessness

While there are many youths who runaway from abusive homes, there are some who choose to leave their families for the freedom and independence of life on the street. They travel around the country and are found in cities such as San Francisco and New York. They consider themselves nonconformists rebelling against what they feel is a corrupt society. According to a recent New York Times article, these youths do not have jobs and often do drugs. They support their habits by stealing, hustling, and begging.

Because these street youths seem to have become homeless just to rebel, there is little sympathy for them. Unlike most homeless people, these teens have the choice to go home, and some do when they run out of money or the weather turns cold.

Jeremy left his home in Maine at seventeen because he was looking for an escape from the small town where he didn't fit in with his punk clothes and dislike of school activities. He came to New York City's East Village, where he ate out of trash cans and slept in the doorways of buildings. For him, street life was about finding his individuality—and about having fun.

After three months on the street, Jeremy tried heroin for the first time. He got sick the next day, but continued to use because it was so easy to get. To get money to buy drugs, Jeremy would steal CDs from the local music store and sell them back to another store. Jeremy's addiction, however, took away his independence. Jeremy was soon arrested for stealing. He didn't want to end up in jail, but it was hard to support his drug habit without the steady flow of money. As winter approached, Jeremy's options became even more limited. He was suffering from withdrawal symptoms. He didn't like sleeping out in the cold. After six months on the streets, Jeremy decided to head back to Maine. His parents welcomed him back, and even helped him get a part-time job. Although Jeremy ended up back home, he will most likely save up his money only to leave again when he has the chance.

SOLUTIONS TO TEEN HOMELESSNESS

Foster Care

The Foster Care Social Services Agency is a national system, regulated by the states, to help, protect, and care for endangered children. Foster care is intended to provide for the temporary needs of homeless children.

Foster homes are regulated by the state for minors whose families are in crisis. Foster parents are paid to provide day-to-day care and to perform the duties of parents. Every minor in foster care is assigned a social worker. The social worker is supposed to keep in close touch with the minor to see that the foster care placement is satisfactory. Unfortunately, some social workers must supervise more cases than they can adequately handle and minors are occasionally placed in overcrowded homes.

In 1997, more than 450,000 children were in America's foster care system, placed there because of abuse, neglect, or other reasons. Most of these children eventually returned to their homes, but nearly 100,000 did not. Typically, children remain in foster care three or more years while waiting to be adopted into permanent homes. President Clinton hoped to increase adoption of children in foster care by giving the families a break on their taxes. His goal was to double the annual 27,000 adoptions each year of foster-care children to 54,000 by the year 2002.

Foster care is designed to provide a temporary solution to children's homelessness. Foster care should never replace children's homes for their entire childhood. The 1997 tax break legislation was designed to address this type of situation. When a teen is abused, neglected, or abandoned, he or she is at risk of homelessness. Some are put into foster care before that happens. A social worker or a school counselor may recognize the warning signs and arrange for the teen to be put into foster care. It can be difficult to adjust to a new home, a new set of surrogate parents, and new rules to follow. It can also be hard because a teen is now responsible for his or her behavior. Prior to foster care placement, a homeless or at-risk of homeless teen was probably not accustomed to following any set pattern of behavior.

Peter's family had no rules. As long as no one called to complain, his parents didn't care what he did. Peter ate whatever there was in the house. He had no curfew. He had no extra clothes. What little he had, he usually stole. When Peter's parents were around, they went out drinking. They didn't care where he was, or what he did, provided that he created no problems for them. Late one night, Peter and some of his friends robbed a convenience store and ran away. A car struck Peter and broke his back. Peter's mother was out on the town, and it was a couple of days before she finally came home. After almost a year in the hospital, Peter was placed in a foster home.

"The rules. That is the hardest part about a foster home," says Peter. "Now I see things differently. All these rules are to help me. My bus comes last, so I have the bathroom last in the morning. It is hard for me to get around, so everyone else has to be up and dressed before me. My foster brother, Doug, complained at first. The rules seemed to center around me, and it made me very self-conscious, but I can see why we need them."

Doug arrived at the foster home two years after Peter. Both have now lived there for more than five years. Doug too had trouble with the rules. "Peter is right," says Doug. "The rules were a pain. When I came here, I couldn't get out the window at night. Peter's bed was in front of the window, so he was in the way. Deep inside, I was glad. I saw what sneaking out and running around had done to Peter. I always thought I would die as part of a gang or something, because I had no real future. Part of me misses the freedom of being with my friends, but the other part of me sees the light at the end of a very dark tunnel. I think now I really have something to look forward to. The strange part is that even my gang had rules. As wild and mean as we were, we still had rules. Now I'm the only one going anywhere. Two of my friends are dead from gang shootings. Another is in a coma at a hospital, and I think the rest are locked up in juvenile detention."

Living in a structured environment has given Peter and Doug a new life. For people to get along, there must be rules for what is acceptable and what is not acceptable. There must be a time to eat, a time for school, a time for chores, and time to just hang out and have fun. Having responsibilities is part of belonging to a real family. Everyone must do their share.

Foster parents are people who like helping others. They are not paid a lot for what they do. Money is not their reason for being foster parents. Some foster parents may not have children of their own and want to share their home. It takes six months to a year to become a foster parent. Foster parents must go through extensive training and attend special classes. Not everyone is appropriate to be a foster parent and there are some requirements that every foster parent must meet. Becoming a foster parent depends on the following:

— age
— income and ability to handle money
— the number of children living in the house
— the size and safety of the home
— access to suitable transportation
— health
— a clean background (letters of reference from both relatives and nonrelatives are required)

If the foster parents meet all of these requirements, they then must take the special training course. Some teens have special problems, so foster parents are allowed to choose the type of problems that they can handle. Even though the requirements may be different from state to state, these are basically the expectations of a foster parent. A foster parent must think you are very important to go through the difficulty of qualifying. A foster parent is not trying to replace a natural parent. When foster parents take on the responsibility of caring for a foster teen, they know that the natural parents have had difficulty providing care. Their only desire is to help a foster teen find the road to success.

When a teen is place in foster care, he or she may have questions, such as: Will my new family like me? Will I like them? How different will it be from my old home? Can my brother or sister come with me? The best solution is to keep an open mind and talk about how you feel. Try not to make quick judgments about your foster care family. It will take time for you and your family to adjust to the new situation. Try to talk to your foster parents about your fears and expectations. By sharing your feelings, you can begin to build a trusting relationship. Trust is an essential element to the success of your foster care experience.

If possible, foster teens are placed with families of their same ethnic background. Being with a family similar to your own background can ease the transition. Unfortunately, due to the lack of available homes, this does not always happen.There are many rules that states apply to foster homes, including how many teens one home can take in. This may force you to be split from your siblings. It is difficult to be apart from your family, but a brother or sister can come to visit you.

Many teens end up running away from their foster care families. But even for teens who find themselves with uncaring foster parents, running away is never the answer. Running away only makes your problems worse by putting you back on the streets. If you are unhappy in your situation, talk with your case worker and ask to be placed in another home. Vanessa decided to give her foster parents a chance. She realized that by trusting them, she would be able to continue her education and eventually, move on with her life.

Homeless minors are the hardest age group to place in foster care or adoptive homes. Teens who have run away from many foster families are sometimes placed in group homes. Homeless adolescents and teens who stay on the streets have a very hard time developing the necessary social skills or work skills that enable them to reenter mainstream society. There is help available if you find yourself at risk. The help list at the end of this book will provide you with resources to prevent or help you address homelessness.

Group Home Living

Sometimes, teens who have runaway or are abused are not successfully placed in a foster family. Sometimes, the foster family cannot handle them, and asks that they be removed. Extremely troubled teens have difficulty adjusting to having new rules and new parents. And sometimes, the foster family continues the pattern of abuse and a teen thinks that life on the street is better than another abusive homelife.

The Department of Social Services recognizes that there are some teens who need a different kind of environment to grow and succeed. These types of teens are put into group homes. These homes are all-male or all-female and have many rules that the residents must follow. One particular home for homeless teens in Boston houses as many as ninety-five girls at a time.

The goal of group homes is to educate the teens and give their chaotic world some structure and sense. When a girl in the Boston Group Home tries to run away, a staff member will follow her everywhere she goes until she agrees to come back. Staffers at this group home say most of the runaways return. Staffers are very committed to the teen residents. Some residents stay in the group home for a few years until they are ready to live on their own, or are able to commit to a foster family.

Stephanie was in sixth grade when she first experimented with drugs and alcohol. All her friends smoked pot and drank booze, so when she hung out with them drinking or smoking pot was the "in" thing to do. By eighth grade, she and her friends shoplifted regularly to get money to buy drugs and alcohol. Stephanie began to experience mood swings both at home and at school. She acted out often with teachers and peers at school. She threw tantrums at home and screamed and yelled whenever her parents tried to talk with her.

Stephanie's grades began to slip, and when her midterm reports showed several failing grades, her parents grounded her for two weeks. When Stephanie's two weeks were up and she was finally allowed to attend a party, it turned out to be pretty dull—until a group of older boys crashed the party. They brought liquor, drugs, and lots of exciting ideas. After a few joints and several beers, Stephanie was feeling pretty fearless. When one of the boys Keith dared Stephanie to run off with him in his van, she didn't hesitate to accept his offer. Leaving her troubled life behind sounded exciting. Stephanie assumed she could escape from her problems and never look back.

Stephanie went home late that night to pick up a few clothes and leave a note for her sleeping parents. She left without giving her future a second thought. Three days later, Stephanie could not have been more sorry. Keith became abusive when he drank too much, which was most of the time. He abused her both physically and emotionally. So that night while Keith slept, Stephanie ran away again.

She was tired, but so confused and hung over that she didn't even consider returning home. When a man offered her money for sex the next morning, Stephanie accepted to get a hot meal and a warm shower. At first, Stephanie was so thrilled with the money she earned that she ignored the dangers surrounding her. But when Stephanie was not with a customer, she had no place to stay. She was on the streets. She carried her few belongings in a backpack. Once, while Stephanie slept on a park bench, someone tried to steal the shoes right off her feet. Stephanie often went to a fast-food restaurant or a gas station to use the rest room. Sometimes she got mugged and robbed of her money.

One afternoon, while Stephanie slept in an alley, she was raped and cut badly by her assailant. If a policeman had not found her by chance, she probably would have bled to death. He took Stephanie to a nearby clinic for treatment. During her stay at the clinic, Stephanie became free of alcohol and drugs. Now that Stephanie could think clearly, she was scared and totally depressed. She wondered how her life became so awful. Yet deep down, Stephanie knew that she had allowed drugs and alcohol to mess up her judgment. Running away from home had ruined what was left of her life. Because of her age, Stephanie had to agree to go into a group home or contact her parents. When she called home, her mother hung up on her.

At the group home, Stephanie met two other female runaways who convinced her to go back to school or work for a GED diploma. Stephanie accepted the house rules established by the home and for the first time in years, Stephanie felt optimistic about her future.

Unfortunately, many teens have to take on too much responsibility too soon. In a recent Gallup Youth Survey, 32 percent of teens reported worrying about staying healthy in the future as well as having enough food to eat. Even worse is that these worries are becoming a reality for young people. Remember, if you are homeless or at risk, reach out to the community services available to you. The last chapter in this book can give you advice on how to cope with your situation, as well as practical advice on how to break the cycle of homelessness.

CHAPTER 5

Homelessness: Finding Options and Dealing with Feelings

F or many, it's difficult to imagine living with only whatever you can carry. Could you survive with no place to sleep, no phone, no mail box, and few personal belongings? Tens of thousands of homeless people live without the security that most of us take for granted. They have no comforts. They have no security or safety. Each day is a struggle.

How will we get food and water? How will we find a bathroom, or a shower? What will happen to me or my family? Teenagers ask these questions when they face homelessness for the first time. Will my family be able to stay together? Will I ever see my friends again? Will we find a place to sleep? Will others harm us to avoid sharing space with newcomers? Too often the homeless must scrounge in garbage dumpsites to find food to eat. Many times they do not eat at all and live with constant hunger. They may sneak into public rest rooms to wash their hands and faces or to quickly rinse out a piece of clothing.

Physically, the homeless suffer from the effects of over-crowding, poor nutrition, and stress from being uprooted. Some end up living in places like garages or basements. Others stay in tents or abandoned shacks with no heat, water, or bathrooms. They live in filthy conditions for years merely to have a roof over their heads. They fight off the weather and other toxic elements that constantly threaten what little protection they have found.

Homeless children often do not get proper immuniza-tions against childhood diseases. Taking trips to the doctor for shots and keeping accurate medical records of them are difficult for the homeless. Chronic health problems like allergies, and hearing, vision, or dental problems often go untreated or without proper follow-up. The com-plications of untreated illnesses often interfere with a child's learning and growth development. The homeless also have no place to prepare food. They rely on junk food or fast foods when they can afford to buy a meal. Many people skip meals regularly. This makes it nearly impos-sible to follow a special diet when necessary. Improper nutrition is even more dangerous for growing children and pregnant women.

Besides the daily pressure of meeting physical needs, the homeless also carry a heavy emotional burden. Feel-ings of failure, shame, despair, anger, and depression are very common. Many teenagers are angry at their parents or at society for disrupting their lives and making them homeless. They often grieve for the life and possessions they left behind. Depression, loneliness, and worry about the future cause some of the homeless to lose hope. This type of depression is understandable and real. Without help or treatment, however, it compounds the problem.

If you are homeless or at risk of homelessness, it's natural to feel afraid for your family and your future. You wonder who will take care of you or if you will be separated from your family. You may be scared that you will be homeless forever. It can be difficult to answer all these questions, however, because the circumstances surrounding every situation are different. We will examine some of the more common solutions to the problems of homelessness. Hopefully, you will find the answers you need to successfully cope with your condition.

HOUSING OPTIONS

Staying with Relatives or Friends

If you and your family have recently become homeless, and it's likely the situation is only short-term, you may find shelter with a relative or family friend. Often a grandparent or an aunt or uncle will agree to take you and your family in for a short while. It can depend on the size of your family and the financial status of your relatives. Sometimes, even though a relative wants to help, he or she does not have enough room or money to help your family. You may be sent to a relative's house by yourself, while your parent looks for work and tries to get the family back on its feet. It's difficult to suddenly find yourself living in someone else's home without your parents, but hopefully in time you will be back with your family.

Dawn's father lost his job when the company he worked for merged with another company. Dawn, age fourteen, understood that she and her father would need to cut expenses. They stopped eating out and going to the movies. Dawn offered to get a part-time job, but her father said he didn't want her to do that. She was too young. A month later, her dad's car broke down and he could not afford to fix it. Dawn's father had trouble getting to job interviews by bus. Their money was running out, and her dad could not pay the next month's rent.

Dawn called her mother, who lived in another state with her new husband and four children. Her mom said they did not have room for Dawn but that Aunt Melanie might let Dawn stay with her for a while. Dawn moved to her aunt's house and her father went to a shelter. Aunt Melanie and her family treated Dawn well, but she felt lonely and anxious. She wondered what would happen if her father could not get a job soon. She worried about his safety in the shelter. She missed him and hoped they would be together soon.

The next week Dawn enrolled in school and felt better about her situation. She helped with the dishes and housework and baby-sat her young cousins. But she found it hard to sleep in a bedroom with her cousins ages one, three and four. She rarely slept a night without one of them fussing or crying. Dawn hoped her housing situation would not last forever. She knew her dad would eventually find a job so they could live as a family again. Meanwhile, Dawn tried to remain cheerful and optimistic.

When you move in with a relative, you usually encounter a lot of changes, even if you stay in the same town. First, you're in a different house. Maybe you have to share a bedroom. You might not even have a room—only a couch to sleep on. If you have to move any distance, you'll probably have to change schools and adjust to new teachers and a new school atmosphere. But the greatest changes come from living with different people and different rules, and the difficulty of trying to fit into a new family.

Shelters

Shelters provide temporary beds, food, and counseling. Most shelters do not allow people to stay longer than thirty days. Shelters are found in most cities and may be run by the city or by private charities. The accommodations vary greatly from city to city.

Shelters are often the last resort for some families. They want to avoid dealing with case workers and the complex forms and requirements necessary when applying for space at a shelter. Since shelters are meant to be short-term housing, they often lack the comforts of a permanent home.

After admittance to a shelter, the homeless are frequently transferred to other shelters. This instability makes it difficult for children to attend school and becomes an additional stressor for all family members.

Shelter living can be difficult. Many shelters have strict rules you must follow. Many routine tasks, such as when you can use the phone or take a shower, are regulated. Some shelters provide food, some don't. There may not be enough food to eat and no place to cook.

Some shelters lack privacy and are overcrowded. It is unlikely that you will find a place of your own to think or relax. There may be no place to keep private things from being stolen. Noise and the lack of privacy can make it extra hard to do homework. It seems that everything you do can cause more stress.

Other problems that exist include the spread of sickness and disease. Since families are living in such close quarters, it's easier to get sick.

Many homeless people object to the rules and routine that shelters establish. Typical rules are:

- You must sign out if you leave and sign in when you return.

If you do not return by 7:30 PM, you will not be allowed back in.

- You must make your bed and your childrens' beds neatly.
- Parents must supervise children at all times.
- No visitors are allowed.
- No food, drinks, or radios are allowed in sleeping areas.
- No perishable food is allowed; no cooking is permitted.
- TV time is 7:00–10:00 PM.
- Bedtime for all children is 9:00 PM.
- Quiet hours are 10:00 PM until 8:00 AM.

Typical Shelter Daily Schedule:

6:15 AM	Wake up
8:00 AM	Leave shelter
11:00 AM	New registration
5:00 PM	Dinner
7:00 PM	Doors closed
9:30 PM	Get ready for bed
10:00 PM	Lights out

Although rules and schedules are necessary when housing large numbers of people, you can see how people might feel restricted and object to them. Some shelters are not safe. Overcrowding causes discontent, and fighting and violence is a constant threat. You have already read about other homeless people and you may encounter different kinds of people in a shelter. Some may be mentally ill, some may be abusing drugs.

But not all shelters are unpleasant. Some shelters, usually ones privately run by churches and civic groups, offer a clean and safe atmosphere. Many times, these shelters see more homeless people needing assistance than they can accommodate. They do not have enough resources to offer more than brief relief from the streets.

Welfare Hotels

Welfare hotels offer a little more privacy than shelters. Families may have to share a bathroom with other families, but they usually have at least one room to themselves. Usually, there are long waiting lists for these accommodations.

The average stay in a welfare hotel may vary from several days to a year, making it a more long term option. Most welfare hotels, however, are in bad condition, with crumbling walls and broken toilets. In most cases, the hotels are located far away from the homeless family's roots, making the family feel even more isolated from mainstream society.

Federally Assisted Housing

Only about one in three families living below the poverty level lives in federally assisted housing. The waiting lists are long, and conditions in these housing projects are often not safe. Drug dealers and prostitution are big problems in many housing projects. Many of the projects built in the 1970s are now in dire need of repair. Large numbers of these buildings are being torn down, and newer buildings are slowly replacing them.

Wesley grew up in low-income housing, or projects, with his mother and his brother. Wesley was eleven when he began selling drugs, a fairly accepted behavior around his building. His mom worked as a day care provider and did not come home until 7 o'clock. Wesley and his brother grew up as "latchkey kids," who came and went as they pleased.

Wesley's father, who never married his mother, dropped out of sight shortly after Wesley was born. But his older brother, Spike, showed him the ropes. When Spike was fifteen, he was arrested for selling cocaine to an undercover police officer. He served six months in prison. Those six months changed Wesley's life. His mother had always been aware of the purse—snatching and muggings around the projects. But now she realized that if Wesley did not reform, he, too, would end up in trouble with the law.

"You're going to change your ways." she insisted. "I'm not going to let you ruin your life, too!"

Wesley, who was diabetic, was afraid to do drugs. Although he pushed drugs under Spike's direction, he was never deeply involved. Because he was Spike's brother, the gangs left him alone. But Wesley knew that while Spike was in jail, his protection was limited. His mother was right. He needed to change his behavior.

"Don't get so excited, Mom," Wesley said. "I'm still in school. I'm not running around at night. If I don't push the drugs for Spike, we'll be hurting for money," Wesley pointed out.

"I don't want drug money. I want you to stay clean. The YMCA where I work has a job opening for a pool assistant. I want you to apply for it. I know they will hire you."

Wesley promised himself to behave more responsibly. Since Spike's arrest, he had done a lot of thinking. His mother really needed him, so he applied for and got the YMCA job. He spent his afternoons keeping their swimming pool clean.

Everything fell into a routine pattern until Spike came back home. He was angry and moody, and he argued constantly with his mom about dealing drugs. But that did not last long. A week later, Spike was shot and killed after a dispute with another drug dealer. Although Wesley and his mother knew that gang members were responsible for Spike's death, the police did not have enough evidence to charge them. Now Wesley and his mom are working hard to earn enough money to move to better housing. Wesley's mom attends night school two nights a week to earn her GED diploma. Wesley goes directly from school to his job at the YMCA. He stays home at night to do homework and does not hang out on the streets.

He makes good grades and his school counselor thinks Wesley has a good chance of earning a college scholarship. Despite all the hardships, Wesley copes well with his near homelessness and is determined to work towards a promising future.

DEALING WITH FEELINGS

Stress

Being homeless or at-risk of homelessness can cause much stress in your life. Stress can affect your school, your mood, and your health. You may feel like it is point-less to worry about your education when you are strug-gling to find food to eat or if you are being separated from your family. The stress of keeping your problem a secret can feel overwhelming.

Stress is extra pressure and demands made on the mind and body. Everyone feels stress and each of us must learn to live with stress. Being homeless increases the amount of stress in your life. It can be embarrassing to reveal your situation to a friend or teacher. But talking about your problems can remove some stress from your life. It's important to find ways to feel good about yourself even when your life seems to be falling apart. Making an effort with your schoolwork can help improve your self-esteem. Working towards a solution can give you the hope you need to move on. There are resources available to you and your family.

You can learn to manage your stress. How stressful your life is partly depends on how you react to the pressure. If you learn to control the way you react, the better you learn to manage your stress. In this way, stress can work for you instead of against you. It can help you become a more productive person, which will help you feel better about yourself and your situation.

Myths and Truths About Stress:

Myth: The best way to deal with stress is to remove it from your life.

Truth. Stress is a permanent part of life. It will not go away. The best way to deal with it is to learn how to manage it, make it work for you, not against you.

Myth: Nervous people lead stressful lives.

Truth: Some people are more prone to stress than others, but anyone can learn to manage stress. Your circumstances can add to the stress in your life, but anyone can learn to manage stress. If you are homeless or at-risk of homelessness, it doesn't mean you will always be overwhelmed with stress.

Myth: Strong people don't let stress get them down.

Truth: Stress is not a sign of weakness. Stress is a part of every person's life. Adults as well as teens have problems with stress and must learn how to manage it.

Myth: Once you learn the rules, managing stress will never be a problem.

Truth: Every kind of stress is different. Managing stress with your living situation and with your parents is different from dealing with stress with your friends and teachers at school. What works in one situation may not work in another. Learning the tools to deal with one kind of stress will help you manage other kinds of stress as well.

When the human body is under constant stress, it gets weak. The longer a person suffers from stress, the greater his or her chances are of getting sick. A body under a great amount of stress becomes exhausted very quickly. You may feel constantly tired. Simple tasks and decision become overwhelming to you.

Feelings that Add to Stress

Anger is a natural and healthy emotion. You may feel angry at your parents for causing your homelessness. You may be angry at the world for ruining your life. It's important to deal with your anger in a healthy way. You may feel that whoever is to blame should fix the problem. It's not that easy, however. You may be right that the situation is not fair, but if you are homeless, it's necessary to deal with your feelings in a positive way to make your life better. Avoiding your feelings, or engaging in destructive behavior, will only makes things worse.

Homelessness can make you feel powerless. It's frustrating to feel like you have no control over your situation. You may do things to try and improve your life, but nothing seems to work. You could feel like giving up, or engaging in unhealthy activities, such as drugs. It's important to vent your frustration and learn that while there are some things you can't control, there are things in your life that you can make better.

Homelessness can make you feel afraid if you don't know what's going to happen. When you lose the security of your home, you start to worry about many other things. Unfortunately, being homeless forces you to worry about things you may have previously taken for granted, like food and privacy and safety. Now, you may worry about the dangers of the shelter or housing where you live. Ask questions, talk to counselors. The more you know, the less you will feel afraid.

These are some of the feelings teens face when they are homeless. There are no easy answers to your problems, but the best way to cope with your feelings is to talk about them. There are counselors available to help you sort through all the different feelings and emotions you have. There is also a help list at the end of this book that provides hot lines and organizations that you can call.

Find a trustworthy person to talk to. If you are with your family, confide in a parent. If you are alone in your situation, even if it is embarrassing, talk to a close friend. A good friend will listen and help you through your situation. Sometimes it's easier to talk to a peer. Talk to a guidance counselor or a teacher at school. Try writing down your thoughts in a journal. Talking to someone will make you feel less alone, and taking back some control will help you feel better about yourself and your life.

Changing Your Behavior

Don't try to be all things to all people. It's important to be honest with yourself. You may decide to do whatever you can to remedy your situation, but you're only one person. You can't do it all. Recognize when to slow down. Otherwise you may create more stress in your life than is necessary. For example, maybe it's too much to try and get straight As, hold down a job after school, volunteer at a teen hot line, and excel on the school's track team. Doing all of this would be difficult for anyone. If you are dealing with an unstable home life, it can become so overwhelming that you give up on everything.

It's also important to judge your risks. It's true that if you don't take risks, you don't make progress, but you need to ask yourself how important the activity really is. Maybe it's worth the added tension and stress, maybe it isn't. At this time in your life, you need to weigh the risks carefully. Sometimes it's beneficial to take a calculated risk. It can be worth it to confide in a friend and tell them about your home life. Your friend may judge you, but he or she may also be a good listener who can help you through this difficult time. Sometimes, though, the risk is foolish, such a joining a gang because you think it will provide you with stability in your life.

It can be difficult to think positively when you face losing your home. It's easy to believe life stinks and nothing is ever going to change. Always seeing the dark side of things increases the stress in your life and can cause depression. But being homeless does not mean your life is over. It may be out of your control at the moment, but it won't feel that way forever. Try to focus on the things over which you have control. If there is nothing you can do to change your situation, accept that. But also try and look for other ways to make your life more positive.

CHAPTER 6

Problems Homeless Teens Face

Homelessness is often accompanied by many other problems. Homelessness is a major life upheaval, and certain situations can compound the problem. By recognizing them, you can work to avoid difficulties that may prevent you from recovering from your circumstances and moving on with your life.

Drug Abuse

Homelessness can cause young people to turn to drugs. Drugs may seem like a good way to relieve stress and forget about your problems. Living on the streets may expose you to the threat of drugs, and you may feel that getting involved with them is no big deal. But drugs will only make your problems worse. Abusing alcohol, cocaine,

72

heroin or crack leads to addiction. Addiction to drugs or alcohol will cause major problems in your life. Stopping an addiction is very difficult. Dealing with homelessness is hard enough, without the added problem of drug addiction.

There are different stages of drug abuse and addiction. Not everyone becomes an abuser or an addict when they take drugs. But many people cannot control their drug use. Some people are more likely to become addicted than others. It is important to know the risks before you start experimenting with drugs. Some research suggests that drug addiction is genetic. That is, you may be at a higher risk for drug abuse if your parents abuse drugs. Drug addiction is a disease. If someone in your family suffers from drug addiction, it does not automatically make you an addict. But your chances of developing an addiction are increased. It's something to be aware of *before* you take any drug.

Often, when a teen starts using a drug, he or she doesn't think it will become a problem. You may believe that you can handle it. Your friends may pressure you into trying drugs. You may start using them to fit in with a certain crowd on the street or at school. They may tell you that drugs won't hurt you. That is wrong. Taking drugs is dangerous and can lead to abuse and addiction.

You may try a drug because someone tells you it will make you feel good. You may try a drink or take a pill because you feel uncomfortable or nervous and need to relax. You may think it's safe because everyone else is doing it. But taking drugs is not safe. Using any drug, even once, can be dangerous. If you continue taking drugs, your body soon develops a tolerance to them. For example, at first, a couple of drinks may be all you need to feel good. But soon you find that you need much more than that to have the same feeling. The longer you use a drug, the more you will need to increase the amount.

What begins as casual use becomes a common occurrence. Soon, the drug use progresses and becomes a habit. Drugs are always around and a part of every activity. When a person begins to lose control over how much or how often drugs are used, he or she has crossed the line into abuse. Drugs become more and more important in an abuser's life. At this stage, drugs start to cause major trouble in your life. The longer a person abuses a drug, the greater the chance that he or she will become addicted.

Addiction means completely losing control over how much you use or how often you use. When a person is addicted to drugs, he or she cannot stop using. Addiction results from physical and psychological dependence. Psychological dependence means that a person *thinks* he or she needs the drug in order to function. An addict believes it's impossible to get through the day without taking the drug, and often thinks that he or she functions better when using the drug. Physical dependence means that a person's *body* needs the drug to function and experiences withdrawal symptoms without it. The body becomes accustomed to the drug and an addict, without the drug, feels sick and experiences one or more of the following: nausea, sweating, confusion, depression, insomnia, chills, cramps, and disorientation.

An addict cares only about getting drugs and maintaining the supply. Everything and everyone in an addict's life means less than the drug. An addict cannot stop using on his own and needs professional help to quit. An addict causes many problems not only in his or her own life, but also in the lives of family and friends. Teen drug abuse is a growing problem. Teenagers are encountering drugs at younger ages than ever before. Teens start using drugs for various reasons. Whether it is because you feel unsure of yourself and look to drugs for confidence, or you're curious and want to rebel, taking a drug is not the answer to any problem. If you are living on the streets, drugs will be more readily available. You may decide to take drugs just because they are there and you want an escape from your life.

Drugs alter your personality in many ways. One common change is a loss of your inhibitions. Inhibition is an internal force that controls certain activities and expressions. It may feel good to lose your inhibitions because you think you feel more relaxed and confident on them. But you may end up doing things you wouldn't normally do. Inhibitions can be good. They can act as warning signals that help us decide what we feel comfortable doing. When our inhibitions are gone, we may not fully weigh the consequences, or possible outcomes, of our actions.

Rebellion and experimentation are rites of passage for most teens. But it's important to be careful. Trying drugs just to see what it feels like can be very dangerous and can lead to serious problems in your life. Making poor decisions because of drugs can also cause permanent damage to your future life. Drugs can prevent you from achieving goals and realizing your dreams. If you find yourself turning to drugs or if you are pressured to try them, talk to a counselor at school or a parent, or call a drug hot line. It is worth the effort to stay away from drugs. If you are homeless, you need to spend your time working on ways to recover from your situation. Doing drugs will only set you back further in your quest to get back on your feet.

Joining a Gang

Being homeless can make you feel very alone, especially if you have run away or are living on the streets without any family for support. Gangs claim to be "surrogate" families for many young people. But the promised loyalty of a gang family can force you to commit acts of violence in return. Many gangs routinely steal from others, deal drugs, even murder members of rival gangs. Once you've joined a gang, it is extremely difficult to get out. Gangs put you and your future at risk. You could end up in jail or lose your life to an enemy gang member. Gangs may seem appealing when you are living on the streets, but there are better ways to help yourself. Joining a gang only makes it harder in the end to take control of your life.

The use of guns is quite common in gangs and most gang shootings involve other gang members. Since a gang's main duty is to protect its turf, simply wearing another gang's colors on a gang's turf is reason enough to be killed. The killing of a gang member usually provokes a revenge killing, and so on.

Many teens think they can join a gang and then leave when the trouble starts or when they want to move on with their lives. But it's not that simple. When you leave a gang, it's members treat you like an enemy. You may be watched because your old gang members think you will tell people their secrets. You may be killed for being a risk. Gangs can make you feel important and make you feel that you belong, but it is not worth the risk of ending up in jail or losing your life.

Almost every gang breaks some law routinely. It may be as minor as vandalism, such as spray-painting a gang's symbol on buildings, or as serious as theft, or murder.

Many gangs engage in drug dealing to make money. Drug dealing is also dangerous gang work. You must always be on guard and you are in constant danger of being killed. Sometimes, drug dealers make more money than they would otherwise, but it's not worth giving up your freedom and ruining you future for a life of gangs and drugs.

The above-mentioned activities are not only harmful, but are against the law as well. If you break the law, you can go to a juvenile detention center or to jail, even if you are still a minor. Having a criminal record will affect the rest of your life. It will make it more difficult for you to continue your education and get a job. Without a good education or a job to support yourself, your chances of continuing the cycle of homelessness are high. Due to the rise in crime by young people, many courts are giving harsher punishments to juveniles. Even if you are under 18 years old, you may be facing jail time for drug abuse.

Sexually Transmitted Diseases

Teens living on the streets sometimes turn to prostitution as a way to make money and survive. However, selling your body is a terrible way to live. It may seem like a way to take control over your life, but it only makes you dependent on the people who pay for sex. Prostitution often leads to drug abuse. Addiction to drugs can force a person to continue a life of prostitution to support a drug habit. This cycle becomes increasingly difficult to escape. Prostitution can also put you at risk of contracting a sexually transmitted disease (STD). While some STDs, such as herpes, gonorrhea, and chlamydia, can be treated, AIDS (Acquired Immune Deficiency Syndrome) has no cure and can be fatal.

More than 2,000 teens get syphilis or gonorrhea every year. Thousands of teens each month discover they are infected with the AIDS virus. About half of all the people in America who have STDs are 25 years old or younger. The more you learn about STDs, the better you are able to protect yourself against them. STDs are highly infectious. Many have similar symptoms. They spread by sexual contact and can affect the penis, vagina, rectum, anus, and other organs. STDs are very dangerous if they are not treated.

There are ways you can reduce the risks of contracting a STD. Make it a habit to use a condom every time you have sex. Condoms reduce the chance of transmitting a disease as well as reduce the risk of pregnancy. Some people don't want to bother using a condom because they are embarrassed or they are afraid that their partner will not like it. But a condom will keep you from getting AIDS. It's crucial that you protect yourself and insist on using a condom even if you have a reluctant partner. That's why it's important to know your partner. Each person that your partner has had sex with increases the chance that he or she has a disease, which increases your chances of getting it. Knowing the sexual history of your partner can help you protect yourself.

It's also important to be aware of your own body. Look carefully at your body and know what it looks like normally. Pay attention to how you feel as well as how you look. Keep an eye out for any changes in your body. Certain changes could be caused by a STD, in which case you should see a doctor as soon as possible. Many STDs are transmitted unknowingly. If you don't know you have a STD, you can spread the disease to someone else and not be aware of it. While it is crucial to use a condom every time you have sex to protect against disease and pregnancy, the only way to be absolutely safe is to abstain from sex altogether.

Some people think that being HIV-positive is the same thing as having AIDS. It's not. HIV is short for human immunodeficiency virus. Someone who is immunodeficient does not have enough of the kinds of cells needed to protect the body from infections and diseases. People find out they have HIV by having their blood tested. The test measures the immune cells that try to combat HIV. Testing positive for HIV means that those immune cells showed up in the results and that you have the virus in your body. You can feel perfectly fine and healthy for a very long time when you are HIV positive. Having AIDS, on the other hand, means you have some kind of illness, or series of illnesses, because your body no longer has what it needs to fight off disease or infection. Probably one of the scariest things about AIDS is that it is hard to predict what kind of illness will hit you and when.

If you are HIV-positive, you may already know or be able to guess how you got it. HIV is transmitted through contact with infected semen, vaginal fluids, or blood, or it is passed from mother to child during pregnancy or childbirth. It is very important that you learn how to prevent the virus from spreading. This is true for two reasons: protecting others and protecting yourself. Even if you are already infected, you can become re-infected by someone else who is HIV-positive, which may weaken your immune system more. It's in your own best interest to avoid the transmission of HIV at all costs.

If you are injecting drugs of any kind, you should stop right away. However, if you do continue to inject drugs, at least do it more safely. Don't share needles, clean your needles and syringes with bleach for at least thirty seconds. Blood that is left on the needle or in the syringe can be transferred from one person to another. Even if you are not injecting drugs, they can impair your judgment. Earlier we discussed the loss of inhibitions. If you are engaged in sexual activity and are using drugs or alcohol, you may be less likely to think about safe sex.

For those who are diagnosed with HIV, many feelings may come to the surface: fear, anger, sadness, disbelief, rebelliousness, confusion. These and other feelings are all natural reactions to news that is a shock to the system. People think there must be some mistake, or they go numb because the news is too much to absorb all at once. These are signs of denial. Many people go into denial when they are diagnosed with HIV. They are probably scared and it's natural to push away things that are frightening. If you are dealing with the problems of being homeless as well, you may push it away because it's too overwhelming to think about. Denial can calm you down and you'll feel less stress if you pretend there is nothing to worry about. In the long run, however, being in denial can harm you. You will be less likely to take care of yourself and others if you continue to think you are not infected with HIV. Denial comes from fear, and one way to overcome fear is through knowledge. Learning as much as you can about HIV will take away some of your anxiety. Facing the reality of HIV, without letting it take over your life, will help you continue living and finding purpose in your life.

Many people worry about how others will react to the fact that they have HIV. You may feel ashamed and afraid that others will look down on you. You may worry that you will be rejected by your family and friends. You may, like

Jay, be thrown out of your house when you confide in your family. It's unfortunate, but these concerns are real. Many people think negative things about people with HIV or AIDS. They stigmatize those people without having any valid reason to do so. Some people are judgmental, and they are only concerned with how someone gets the virus. They judge a person's behavior and feel that HIV positive people must have done something to bring the disease on themselves. HIV is a virus, not a sign of bad behavior. No one gets HIV on purpose and no one deserves it. The picture has gotten somewhat brighter. Despite this ignorance and prejudice, there is more general awareness about HIV and AIDS today. With better understanding, people tend to be more sympathetic. You will find people who will act with compassion and sympathy, and show that they love and accept you. Sometimes it may be the ones you least expect. Seek them out. They will help sustain you as much or more than any medication.

When you have HIV or AIDS, you have certain legal rights: the right to keep your status private, the right to agree to HIV testing and treatment, and the right to receive good medical care. Even if you are homeless, these rights still apply to you. Because the exact legal rights vary from state to state, for specific information it's best to call the Department of Public Health or the AIDS hot line in your area. Here are some of the important facts you need to know:

Confidentiality. Because HIV is such a personal matter, and because of the stigma surrounding the disease, confidentiality is extremely important for people with HIV or AIDS. How private you can be about HIV begins with how and where you are tested. When you were tested for HIV, you were either tested anonymously or confidentially. If you were tested at an anonymous testing site, no one knows you by name, and the results were not written down; only a number went on your lab slip. If you were tested confidentially, such as in a doctor's office or clinic, your doctor and possibly other health professionals or staff know your HIV status. They are not supposed to reveal information outside the office without your permission, but they can use the information to begin the proper treatment for you. Generally, most social service and health institutions consider it all right to share information within their organization without getting your permission directly. To talk to a particular person or agency on the outside, they need to ask you first. Then you usually need to sign a release form of some kind. You may want to ask the health or social service agency working with you about your medical records. You should know if HIV information is included in your records and who has access to your records.

Partner Notification. Partner notification refers to telling your sexual or drug partners that they have been exposed to the HIV virus. Laws about sharing this particular information differ among the states. In New York State, for example, partner notification rules are the same for teens as for adults. Your doctor may ask you for the names of people with whom you have had sex or shared needles. He or she will encourage you to tell those persons that you have been tested and are HIV-positive. If you are unwilling to do that, your doctor can notify them that they have been exposed to HIV. He or she cannot reveal your name or tell them how they have been exposed. The only people who are allowed to contact your partners are your doctor or a person you choose to do this for you.

Consent. Most teens under the age of eighteen are considered minors; that is, they do not have the same legal rights or responsibilities as adults. Some decisions you are not allowed to make for yourself as a minor, such as signing a contract or receiving certain kinds of medical care. There are exceptions, however, and some areas of health care dealing with HIV are among them. One exception is having the power to consent or agree to being tested and treated for HIV and AIDS. States have different laws and regulations as to what health-care decisions minors can make. Again, in New York State, any teenager who is considered to have the "capacity to consent" to be tested for HIV (who understands what the HIV test is about) can be tested without an adult's permission. Also, the teen's HIV status cannot be revealed without his or her consent. Exceptions to this include requests for the information from prisons, foster care and adoption agencies, and in child abuse cases. A written consent to reveal HIV-related information is not necessary for health-care providers working in the same institution; however, it is required for any outside agency or facility. Lastly, when it is judged necessary for medical reasons, it is permitted to tell parents or guardians of a teenager's HIV status. This does not mean that you should not consult your parent or guardian; in fact, the opposite is true. However, not all teenagers feel safe confiding in their parents or other adults taking care of them. For teens who are on their own, or who have children of their own, some states have categories called "mature" or "emancipated" minors. There are no definite rules as to who qualifies. Generally, the terms refer to people under the age of eighteen who have a child, live on their own and support themselves, or have been abandoned by their parents or guardians. They are legally able to make certain decisions for themselves. You need legal and social service assistance to become an "emancipated minor."

As you can see, the rules for consent are complex and detailed. Some of the questions to keep in mind about treatment are the following:

What does a "release of information" do in your state?

What services are medical and social service providers permitted to give you without the consent of a parent or guardian?

For what kinds of treatment do you need a parent's or guardian's permission?

No one can be discriminated against because he or she is HIV-positive or has AIDS. This means you cannot:

— be kicked out of school
— be denied medical treatment
— be fired from a job
— be evicted from an apartment solely on the grounds that you have HIV or AIDS.

Most states have a Commission of Human Rights that oversees these laws and can step in when there are violations. Everyone who is HIV-positive or has AIDS has the right to good medical treatment. No one can be denied treatment on the grounds of having HIV or AIDS. It is the law everywhere.

When you are HIV-positive, the first step in taking care of yourself is getting good medical care. Find a doctor that you trust who can take care of both your HIV-related and general medical needs. This can be difficult if you are homeless, but you can find help at an HIV counseling clinic where free medical care may be available. While you are HIV-positive but have no symptoms, your doctor will take care of your primary health-care needs. It is also very important that you try to eat well and sleep well.

You'll need a balanced diet with lots of vitamins to keep your immune system healthy. Again, this can be hard when you are living on the streets, but getting the help you need to take care of yourself will help you stay healthy and keep your T-cell count up. These are the cells in the immune system that are most directly harmed by HIV. The more T-cells you have the healthier you stay. This monitoring is a way of gauging when to start you on certain medicines that will help keep your immune system functioning.

Some general symptoms of HIV illness include night sweats, fevers, extreme fatigue, weakness, and diarrhea, which can lead to loss of appetite and dehydration. There are medications that can offset these and other symptoms. A group of medicines called antivirals are used to fight HIV. These drugs are mostly referred to by their initials: AZT, DDI, and DDC for example. These drugs make it harder to the virus to reproduce itself. One of the most effective and widely used of these drugs is AZT. Many people feel stronger after taking it, gaining weight and energy. It appears to be a major factor in helping people live longer with HIV and AIDS. Some people also experience unpleasant or serious side effects, such as nausea or anemia (low red blood cell count). Your doctor will monitor this if you are treated with AZT or another antiviral medicine. Doctors have been recommending these drugs to treat people with HIV to extend the time before they get AIDS. Recently, this approach has been questioned by some researchers. However, AZT and other drugs are still considered useful against HIV at later stages.

It takes a lot of internal struggle to cope with HIV and AIDS. You may ask yourself questions most people take years to figure out. Talking to a counselor or therapist can be extremely helpful in dealing with strong emotions. These are trained professionals who are completely nonjudgmental. They will listen to you and help you understand your emotions. They may also be able to suggest different ways of dealing with your illness and reducing stress under your circumstances. Support groups for teens with HIV or AIDS are a great way to make you realize that you are not alone. You can share information and make new friends who know what you are going through and will support you through it. Many people find comfort in such a group, a place where they can be themselves.

Sexual Abuse

As we've learned from earlier chapters, many teens runaway from home because of sexual abuse. Unfortunately, runaways may end up in abusive relationships or find themselves engaging in risky behavior to survive on the street. This may lead to a repeat of the sexual abuse from which the teen originally tried to escape. Sexual abuse occurs more often than most people think. It is also more likely to occur with someone you know. It could be a teacher, a coach, a doctor or someone from your own family. The hardest thing about sexual abuse is that is usually happens with someone you trust. This person could be responsible for taking care of you and you may not know what to do when this happens.

Sexual abusers can be violent and use force and threats. A parent may threaten to go away and never come back if the child tells someone what happened. The abuser may also make promises or bribe the child in order to get them to do what they want. Sexual abuse is most likely to happen to a child between the ages of nine and twelve, but a two year old or a seventeen year old can also be a victim of sexual abuse.

Sexual abuse can cause serious problems whether violence is present or not. Teens who are abused feel isolated from their peers. They feel ashamed about what has happened. They may suffer from low self-esteem. Sexually abused teens feel angry and may take that anger out on someone else or they may try to hurt themselves. Some become depressed. The longer the abuse occurs, the more damage it can cause, but if the abuse is stopped early and the teen gets the help he or she needs, the harmful effects of sexual abuse can be prevented. Here are some rules to remember about sexual abuse:

— *Your body belongs to you*. You are the only one who decides how to use your body sexually. In sexual abuse, someone who is older and more powerful decides how to use your body. This is wrong and you have the right to say no.

— *Sexual abuse is never your fault*. You are not responsible for what adults or other people do. Abuse is not your fault, even if you cannot say no to it. Nothing you do excuses another person who uses you for sexual pleasure.

— *Sexual abuse is always harmful*. Sexual abuse always hurts the victim. Sometimes, if the victim is female, she can become pregnant. But the deepest hurt is the way sexual abuse makes the victim feel. These negative feelings can make it hard to succeed in school, have friends, or successfully cope with any other problems.

— *Good people can do bad things*. It is hard to believe that someone you love who is kind to you can sexually abuse you. Abusers may be good people in other ways. They may be gentle when they want to abuse you. But this does not mean the abuse is acceptable. It needs to be stopped.

— *Sexual abuse does not stop by itself.* Sexual abuse is hard to talk about. You may be afraid of your abuser, but the only way to stop the abuse it to tell someone about it and do something about it. There are people who are specifically trained to help and protect you.

— *Keep telling people you trust about sexual abuse until someone listens.* Some adults may not believe you when you tell them about the abuse. You may be told to try and forget about the problem. These are not solutions to the problem. The abuse won't stop by itself. If you find someone doesn't believe you or won't help you, keep trying until you find someone who will.

— *What happens to the sexual abuser is not your fault.* Because sexual abuse is a crime, some abusers go to jail. When the abuser is someone you care about or a member of your family, this is very hard. But only the sexual abuser is responsible for what happens when the abuse is uncovered.

Andrea is twelve years old. She lives with her mother and her seventeen year old brother, Larry in a low income housing project. Andrea's mother works two jobs to support her and Larry. She often works nights and relies on Larry to baby-sit. Andrea and Larry have to share a bedroom because the apartment is so small. The first time Larry bothered Andrea in bed, she was almost asleep. She felt hands on her bottom and she thought it was her mother tucking her in when she got home. The next night she heard Larry cross the room. He sat on the edge of her bed and put his hand in her pajamas. He felt around below her stomach, then he went back to his bed. Andrea lay awake and felt scared.

A week later her brother touched her again. This time Andrea pretended to be asleep. Larry put his hand in her pajamas and started rubbing her genitals. When this happened she felt a tingling feeling and became very confused. She loved her older brother, but she knew what he was doing was wrong. But she also thought it was her fault somehow. Larry continued to sexually abuse Andrea every night. Several times he even got under the covers with her and rubbed his penis against her. She kept her eyes closed and tried to forget what was happening. Outside the bedroom, Larry ignored Andrea.

Andrea started to worry all the time. She felt different from her friends. She stayed by herself, sure that everyone knew about her and Larry. She had trouble in school and started failing some of her classes. One day her friend Maria asked her if something was wrong. Andrea decided to tell her friend. She didn't know what else to do. Maria listened carefully. The next day Maria's mother called Andrea's mother and they talked for a long time. That night Andrea's mother stayed home from work. She made Larry move his bed into the living room. She moved her own bed into the room with Andrea. Even though the family was on a tight budget, Andrea's mother hired Maria's older sister to baby-sit at night. Andrea's mother also called a social worker, who arranged for Larry to get counseling. Hopefully, in time, Andrea would recover from the emotional trauma and Larry would get the psychological help he needed.

Sexual abuse hurts victims physically and emotionally. A number of programs are specially designed to help victims cope. If you have been sexually abused in the past or if you are currently being abused, it will be extremely helpful if you find and participate in one of these programs. Depending upon the circumstances of your abuse, you may wish to participate in a program that is designed to support you alone. Or you may choose a program that will offer support to you and other members of your family.

Post-Traumatic Stress Disorder

Post-traumatic stress disorder is a psychological disorder that can make its victims have difficulty dealing with everyday life. Recognized first in war veterans, PTSD has now been found in victims of nearly any traumatic incident, especially natural disasters. Studies show that about one in four people develop PTSD after a major disaster. The people most likely to develop PTSD are those who have difficulty acknowledging or expressing their emotions. A victim of PTSD experiences a number of emotions ranging from numbness to anger. You may feel disoriented, guilty for having survived when others did not. You may even be depressed. You have lost things that are important to you. Your life may have been totally disrupted. You and your family may not feel in control of your lives and may not for a long time. Your parents may have no jobs to got to and no income for a while. Someone you know may have been hurt or even killed. You and your family cannot tell how things will turn out.

Despite not knowing what will happen, and the fact that you are dealing with all sorts of difficult emotions, you can begin recovering from the shock by taking things one step at a time. First, allow yourself to feel whatever emotions that are milling around inside. Then, work on getting rid of the anger you feel. Try to get enough sleep, but don't be surprised if sleeping well takes time. Think about pleasant memories if you can. You may have trouble remembering things, especially about the disaster, but your memory will improve. You may feel guilty, as though you were to blame for what happened. You were not, but many people make the mistake of taking personal responsibility for negative events. They feel that what they did or did not do during the event was wrong.

People who go through disaster often fear that it will happen again. You may dream about the event. Some survivors of floods have nightmares about water chasing them. They could no longer trust the natural world. It took them a long time to recover. If you feel, as many people with PTSD do, that you simply cannot cope with what has happened, speak to a counselor or a therapist who will help you deal with the emotions brought on by the trauma. There are bad coping strategies, and it's easy to fall into their trap. Mental health workers who have studied the effects of natural disasters on young people say that it is often hard to avoid negative ways of coping. They include:

Distraction. It may take a real effort not to be distracted from your goal of getting your life together again.

Withdrawal. If you are frightened and sad about what has happened, it may seem natural to keep to yourself. It is easier to retreat than to face the future. But you must face it some day. Try to do it now, one step at a time.

Blaming yourself. Blaming yourself for something you did not cause is negative thinking. It can make you depressed. Even if there were things you could have done during the disaster, it is simply not possible to think and act perfectly under terrible conditions.

Blaming others. Even if you think others in your family acted unwisely, the disaster is not their fault. Your family probably did the best they could.

Wishful thinking. "If only . . ." is another way of hiding from reality. Wishing the disaster had not happened may give you a sense of comfort, but the comfort does not last because the bad things really did happen and you will eventually have to deal with them.

You have suffered a loss, perhaps a serious one. Bottling up your emotions can be harmful to you as you try to cope. You must acknowledge and work through these emotions if you are to get over your loss. You can't change what happened, but you can put good, positive coping skills to work for you.

Solving problems. You and your family will have many problems to face after a disaster. To keep from becoming part of the problems, work to be part of the solution. Ask exactly how you can help. Maybe you can sort through damaged belongings, boil water for drinking, baby-sit your little brother, or care for a neighbor's child. By helping others to solve problems, and by keeping busy, you are being both helpful and positive. Tackle things one at a time. Do not try to do too much too quickly. You will feel overwhelmed.

Rebuilding your thinking. It will not be easy to think clearly and positively about the future. It is hard to overcome negative thoughts and memories of the disaster, and you may need outside help in rebuilding your thinking. But you should try to think about getting life back to normal. To help rebuild your thinking:

— Get counseling if you need it.
 Look at the positive side. You are alive. You are
 going to be all right. You can help make things
 better.
— Try not to feel sorry for yourself. You are not the
 only person with problems. Many others may be
 much worse off than you.
— Remember, you can be useful to others.

Reaching out to others. You will help others in your family just by showing your support. Building a bridge to family and friends will help you to recover from the damage everyone has suffered. Find out what has happened to your friends. Help them recover. Let them help you, even if it is only by being your friend. Doing things for others will take your mind off yourself.

As you begin to recover, there may be setbacks for everyone in the family. It may be hard to get life back to normal. When things go wrong, you may relive the disaster and blame it for what is happening. Only a small number of people suffer lasting effects of a disaster and PTSD. Most recover completely. If, however, you find that you are having difficulty recovering, there are people you can talk to. Check with your parent, teacher, guidance counselor, or doctor to find group therapy meetings for PTSD. Recovering from disaster just takes time; how much time depends largely on how badly your life was upset. Remember, you will get your life together. Things will be better. Time is one friend, a positive outlook is another. Believe in yourself and your ability to help yourself. In your mind's eye, picture yourself doing well. The more you "see" yourself happy, the happier you will actually become.

Being a homeless teen is very hard to deal with. There are many different problems and difficult situations to overcome. Homeless teens are at more of a disadvantage than other teens with stable families and homes. Despite this lack of control over certain circumstances, teens can still have some control over what happens to them. Even under great stress, you can try and make smart decisions about your life. Staying in school and staying away from drugs are two important steps in working towards a more positive outlook and life. Setting goals for yourself is an excellent way to help you succeed. It takes hard work, but it can be done. It's also beneficial to ask for help from others when you need it.

CHAPTER 7

Breaking the Cycle

A fter confronting the initial crisis of finding shelter and food, the homeless need to find ways to help themselves. Federal and local social services are available to help solve the problems that lead people to become homeless or nearly homeless. It is necessary to help them find the services necessary to help them get back on their feet.

What skills help people find jobs?

Seventy-five percent of unemployed adults have reading or writing difficulties. More than 27 million Americans are functionally illiterate. They cannot read written directions, street signs, or signs on buses. They cannot get a driver's license, order from a menu, or read a newspaper. They are limited in filling out a job application. Yet, somehow, these people do survive. But another 35 million Americans read below the survival level. They may have dropped out of school or, because of homelessness, have never attended school on a regular basis. Studies estimate that an illiterate adult earns 42 percent less than a high school graduate.

What can you do to help yourself recover from homelessness or to avoid living constantly at risk of becoming homeless? Concentrate on improving your education and job skills. Focus on getting help for any health or mental problems. If your reading and writing skills are limited, ask about literacy programs at your shelter or United Way agency. Also ask at a library or your nearest elementary school. Tutoring or literacy classes can help you improve your marketable skills. Organizations such as Literacy Volunteers of America can help you improve your reading skills free of charge. The elementary school in your neighborhood may have a community program for literacy or be able to direct you to an agency that does have one.

If you did not graduate from high school, see about studying for a high school equivalency diploma, or GED. Libraries and schools offer this information. If you are still in school, get extra help if necessary so you can graduate with skills to help you earn a living. Ask at shelters about social service programs that offer job training. If you are able to get into a program, work hard and learn all you can. If the program helps you find a job, do your best work and continue learning while you work. Getting a part-time job or volunteering in your community can help you gain skills and self-confidence and learn about different kinds of work. You can add these new abilities to the list of qualifications when you write out your resume or fill out a job application in the future.

Create a Support System

A support system is a network of individuals or groups in your life who help you work toward your goals. These people assist you in setting goals, increasing your confidence, and learning new skills. If you are homeless or at-risk of homelessness, a support system can be extremely beneficial to you. The people in your network offer emotional support in good times and bad, and they can also help you find a job, continue your education, and develop your talents. Unfortunately, many teens, especially those in at risk circumstances, do not have a strong support system. Without a network of people around you, you will not be able to meet all your needs. You may feel without direction, lonely, frustrated and hopeless. But you can build a strong social support system for yourself.

Older people can use their experiences to tell you about the choices they have made and the effects these decisions have had on their lives. You may use their advice when you make your own choices.

Joseph used to hang out in Mr. Leone's pizza joint after school everyday. There wasn't much else to do, and he'd rather stay away from the shelter he was living in with his mom for as long as possible. Today was a particularly rough day for Joseph. As he sat sipping his coke, Mr. Leone looked up from the counter and asked him what was on his mind. Joseph was a bit startled. He hesitated a moment, thinking he would just brush him off, but something in Mr. Leone's face made Joseph confide in him. He told him how hard it was living in a shelter, how he didn't have a lot of friends, and he was worried about his future. Once Joseph started to talk, it all poured out. He apologized for talking so much. Mr. Leone just smiled and said he understood. He told Joseph that he was once homeless, but with help he got back on his feet and opened his own restaurant. It was hard and for a long time he didn't think it would be possible, but he did it. Joseph felt relieved and comforted. As he got up to leave, Mr. Leone offered him a part-time job. "Since you hang out here all the time anyway, I should put you to work!"

It isn't always easy to take a chance. Asking other people for help can be scary. But you can get the support you need if you make an effort to reach out. You don't have to pour out your life troubles to everyone you meet, but think about people in your community whom you admire and trust. Very often you'll get a positive response. Many people want to help you, they just don't know you need their support. When you are having a hard time, knowing someone else cares about you can help you go a long way toward overcoming your problems.

Families are a good place for many teens to get support, but sometimes relatives can't or won't help you. If you are struggling with homelessness, sometimes your family doesn't have enough time to provide you with the support you need. You don't have to rely on your family to have a support system. Set up an appointment to meet with a guidance counselor, a teacher at school, a social worker, or a youth leader. Often these people can help you with your problems. They may also be able to suggest other individuals or groups who can become part of your network. If your family belongs to a religious organization, you might contact the priest, minister, or rabbi. Check the local youth center or community club in your neighborhood for teen groups and older mentors. Many communities offer Big Brother/Big Sister programs. Sometimes these programs are advertised at the library or youth center.

If you suffer from mental illness or substance abuse, go to a mental health center to find help. Then stick to the program to help yourself get better. No one can do that for you; you must want a healthier lifestyle and work at it yourself, for yourself.

Stay in School

Several programs are available to help students who are financially at risk but want to stay in school. Consult your school counselor if money problems might cause you to drop out of school.

The Summer Aid Program offers students an opportunity to "earn and learn." The program is for students at least sixteen years old who need financial help or who are disabled. On-the-job training is available. Most summer employees work full-time. The Stay-In-School (SIS) program helps needy or disabled students. To qualify, you must be at least sixteen years old and a full-time student in high school or vocational or technical school. You must have a satisfactory academic record.

In the SIS program, students work for federal agencies while they stay in school. Some of the work assignments include clerks, typists, and laborers. Student aid jobs are also available. The Federal Junior Fellowship Program is for high school seniors. They must have a strong academic record, be planning to attend college and must need financial help. Fellows usually begin work the summer following high school graduation. They work full-time during summers and vacation periods and work part-time during the school year. Fellows often find permanent federal jobs through this program.

GOVERNMENT PROGRAMS

In 1994, President Bill Clinton took action on his campaign promise to "end welfare as we know it." His welfare reform proposal became one of the most radical social policy recommendations since AFDC was created by the New Deal. A record 14.3 million people were on Aid to

Families with Dependent Children in 1994. More than 9 million of the recipients were children. The welfare system did not help most needy people become or remain financially independent.

President Clinton's reform plans provide recipients with health coverage, child care, education and training during their first two years on welfare if they needed it. After that, recipients would be required to work in community service or for private businesses. The plan quickly became known as the "two-years-and-out" plan. Calculations estimated that 1.5 million AFDC recipients would eventually be required to work. In 1996 national welfare reform law ended the federal guarantee of aid to poor families with children. This legislation set a five-year lifetime limit on welfare benefits.

Opponents of the welfare system point out that the present methods of aiding the homeless and the near homeless do not encourage families to remain together. They want to replace welfare with Earned Income Tax Credits for working families. In effect, a worker's income would be increased by a credit on the federal income tax. The added income would raise the wages of a family with one full-time worker to the current poverty level. This earned income credit should not carry the social stigma that welfare does. It would give the recipient greater control of how to use the money.

The verdict is not yet in on the welfare reform debate. Nearly everyone agrees that reform measures are necessary to make current welfare programs more effective. But differing views exits on how best to accomplish this monumental task. Many believe the 1996 welfare reform legislation unfairly affects needy children, the disabled, the elderly, and immigrants. Hopefully, as issues become more focused, something positive will result.

International Programs

The Office of the United Nations High commissioner for Refugees (UNHCR) helps refugees with legal and political aid. The United Nations International Children's Emergency Fund (UNICEF) provides emergency help to children in the least developing nations (Third World countries). UNICEF helps prevent child deaths from disease, malnutrition, and disasters. The U.S. Committee for Refugees (USCR) is a nonprofit, nongovernmental organization. This committee reviews and evaluates the plight of refugees and displaced people worldwide. The USCR works closely with the United Nations in recommending aid for refugees.

The United Nations relief agency and the United Nations High commissioner for Refugees monitor the conditions of refugees. Both agencies airlift food and supplies into warring countries to help refugees. The International Red Cross coordinates emergency relief after natural disasters both in America and Worldwide. The International Committee of the Red Cross (ICRC) serves as a neutral committee in times of conflict. This committee provides food and medical supplies and inspects prisoner-of-war camps. The Salvation Army and the United Way also offer help worldwide as well as nationally.

Other Programs

In 1983, about two-thirds of funding for shelter programs came from charitable sources. Today about one-third of funding for shelters comes from private charities. The remaining two-thirds of funds for shelters comes from federal, state, and local governments. Churches, synagogues, and temples call upon private citizens to donate their time and money, and to help raise funds. Some churches have organized programs to help the homeless find and apply for aid. Many also have programs to direct people to medical clinics, food banks for groceries, or agencies to help with utility bills.

Charities supply free meals at soup kitchens, provide shelters, and distribute food and clothing. Some private organizations offer shelters for battered women, counseling for drug addicts, and on-the-job training. The Salvation Army, the American Red Cross, the United Way, and Second Harvest are active charitable organizations one can contact to locate shelters and soup kitchens. About 25 million Americans a year depend on soup kitchens, food pantries, and other emergency nutrition programs. Approximately 5 million are children twelve years old or younger.

The Transitional Living Grant Program for Homeless Youth is designed to provide residential and other services to homeless teens to help them become self-sufficient. It is an extension of group home living that helps teens who cannot go back to their parents and have no other safe place to go. There are approximately seventy-three transitional living programs federally funded in the United States. The Drug Abuse Education and Prevention Program for Runaway and Homeless Youth give help to youth at risk, hoping to help them avoid time in jails and hospitals.

Moving on with Your Life

Homelessness is often temporary. The average stay of homeless families at shelters is about ninety-five days. The average stay for single men and women is sixty days. While this is a long time for a person living in less than desirable facilities, it is not forever. If you must go to a shelter, think of it as a temporary resource. That is the purpose shelters are intended to serve. The trend in the 1990s is on helping to prevent homelessness. Social programs are available to lend people security deposits and rent money. Utility assistance programs are available to help pay for electricity and heat. Do not hesitate to ask for help when you really need it. If you have problems that might cause you to become homeless, seek help now before it happens.

Homelessness is an active social issue today, and much attention is centered on the plight of the homeless. Currently, many new ideas are being tested. Dehydrated meals, similar to military rations, are being made from surplus crops that were not always harvested. This dehydration method is expected to give food a long shelf life. Such meals could serve many more people at food banks in the near future. An ancient proverb says, "Give a person a fish, and he will eat for a day. Teach a person *how* to fish, and he will eat for a lifetime." Through education and job training, the homeless can learn how to fish, or take responsibility, for themselves. Then they will not need to depend on others to provide for them indefinitely.

Most homeless people need not feel helpless. They need to find the courage to search for solutions to help them regain control of their lives. One should remember that many agencies offer assistance to help people become independent. A homeless or nearly homeless person should not hesitate to call upon community resources when necessary. If a helping hand can enable you to become independent or to cope with a crisis, the government and community are there for you. Learn how to find these agencies when you need help.

Homelessness is about more than people who do not have shelter. Homelessness is about people who do not have or know about resources to help them. Homelessness is about education and family issues. Homelessness is about children and women who are left with little income. People who are homeless or who are vulnerable to becoming homeless need to learn how to make good economic decisions. Quite often, they need a little help from relatives, friends, good neighbors, and agencies who can help them achieve some independence while they are dealing with the events in their lives. As you work on the problems making you vulnerable to homelessness, remember that success is often measured in small steps that seem frustratingly slow. But little is more important than finding solutions to improve the quality of your life.

Glossary

Alcoholic   A person who cannot control his or her consumption of alcohol.

Alcoholic anonymous (AA)   An organization of alcoholics and former alcoholics who support each other to stop drinking.

Counselor   A person who is trained in helping people cope with their problems and develop skills to make changes in their lives.

Detox   Short for detoxification clinic, in which a person is helped to give up drug or alcohol abuse.

Dysfunctional   Not working in the intended way; incomplete, impaired, or abnormal.

Emotional abuse   Having your basic needs of food, shelter, and clothing ignored or neglected. Being denied love or affection or being verbally assaulted and belittled.

Family violence   The mistreatment of one family member by another, including physical, verbal, emotional or sexual abuse.

Foster care   When the state legally takes custody of minors to protect them from abuse or neglect, and places them in the care of paid adults.

Illiterate   Lacking adequate reading and writing skills.

Incest   Sexual contact between family members. Incest is against the law.

Minor   A legal term, referring to a child under the age of eighteen or sixteen. Age varies from state to state.

Poverty   Not having enough money to meet one's basic needs of shelter, food, and clothing.

Refugees People who flee to a different country to escape war, death, or natural disasters.

Runaways Kids fleeing their homes, often because of physical or mental abuse.

Self-esteem How and what we think and feel about ourselves.

Shelters Temporary housing for people who have no permanent place to live.

Social worker A person who works for a community service or other organization that provides aid to people in need of assistance.

Throwaways Youths pushed from their homes or encouraged to leave, often because of drug use or pregnancy.

Where to Go for Help

Check these headings in your telephone book to find private shelters, housing programs, and other local resources:

American Red Cross
Children's Protective Services
Mental Health Centers
Police or 911
Public Health Authorities
Social and Human Services
Social Service Agencies
Welfare Department

Contact local churches, synagogues or social service agencies listed in the Yellow Pages of your local telephone book to find shelters and soup kitchens.

American Red Cross

More than 500 local chapters help the homeless with eviction prevention services, housing vouchers, food, shelter, and emergency services. They also provide free disaster emergency assistance. Check your local telephone book or contact:
American Red Cross
National Headquarters
17th and D Streets, NW
Washington, DC 20006
(202) 639-3610

If there is no Red Cross office near you, contact:
The Federal Emergency Management Agency
P. O. Box 70274
Washington D.C. 20024
Attn: Publications.
Ask for a copy of "Are You Ready?" It also lists many other pub-
lications that deal with specific disasters. These publications are
free. Some are available in Spanish.

Salvation Army

This international religious and charitable organization oper-
ates hundreds of local shelters, soup kitchens, and emergency
services for the homeless. Check your local telephone book or
contact:
Salvation Army
799 Bloomfield Avenue
Verona, NJ 09044
(201) 239-0606

United Way of America

The United Way provides major programs of emergency services including soup kitchens, shelters, food banks, and substance abuse programs for the homeless. Check your local
telephone book or contact:
United Way of America
701 North Fairfax Street
Alexandria, VA 22314-2045
(703) 836-7100

The National Coalition Against Domestic Violence

This agency can direct you to local temporary shelters for battered homeless women. Contact:

The National Coalition Against Domestic Violence
P.O. Box 34103
Washington, DC 20043-4103
(202) 638-6388

WIC

The United States Department of Agriculture (USDA) Special
Supplemental Food Program for Women, Infants, and Children
(WIC). This federally-funded program provides food and nutrition education to eligible pregnant or breastfeeding women,
infants, and children up to five years old. A special food
package is available for the homeless and children and women
with special health needs.
WIC, Supplemental Food Program Division
Food and Nutrition Services
U.S. Department of Agriculture
3101 Park Center Drive, Room 540
Alexandria, VA 22302
(703) 756-3730

Children of the Night

Children of the Night provides a safe haven and shelter to help
sexually exploited teens who are forced into prostitution or
pornography. Located in Van Nuys, CA, this organization provides drug programs, mental health programs, counseling, and
medical care. They also help with GED preparation, court
appearances, finding jobs, finding maternity homes, and rescue
from pimps. After finishing the programs at the shelter, teens
and children are assisted in finding foster homes. Teens also are
helped with independent living arrangements, or with a ticket
home.

24 hour hotline: (800) 551-1300

Hot Line Numbers:

Adolescent Suicide Hot Line	(800) 621-4000
AIDS Hot Line for Teens	(800) 234-TEEN
Al-anon and Alateen	(800) 356-9996
Covenant House	(800) 999-9999
Family Service America	(800) 221-2681
National AIDS Hot Line	(800) 342-2437
National Council on Child Abuse and Family Violence	(800) 222-2000
National Runaway Switchboard	(800) 231-6946
Parents Anonymous	(800) 421-0353
Second Harvest Hot Line	(800) 523-FOOD
National Domestic Violence Hot Line	(800) 333-SAFE
The Clearinghouse on Child Abuse and Neglect Information	(800) 394-3366
National Youth Crisis Hot Line	(800) 442-HOPE
Youth Crisis Hot Line	(800) 448-4663
National Center for Missing Youth	(800) 782-7335
National Center for Missing and Exploited Children	(800) 843-5678
Child Help USA	(800) 422-4453
Child Find Hot Line	(800) 426-5678

For Information:

The National Network of Runaway and Youth Services, Inc.
1400 Eye Street, NW, Suite 330
Washington, D.C. 20004
(202) 783-7949

Adolescent AIDS Program
Montefiore Medical Center
111 East 210th Street
Bronx, NY 10467
(718) 882-0232

Boys and Girls Clubs of America
1230 West Peachtree Street, NW
Atlanta, GA 30309
(404) 815-5700

Children's Bureau Clearinghouse on Child Abuse and Neglect
Information
Department of Health and Human Services
P. O. Box 1182
Washington, D.C. 20013

National Foster Parents Association (NFPA)
P. O. Box 16523
Clayton, MO 63105

Organization of Foster Families for Equality and Reform
P. O. Box 110
East Meadow, NY 11554

National Coalition for the Homeless
National Headquarters
1612 K Street, NW
Washington, D.C. 20006
(202) 659-3310

Habitat for Humanity International, Inc.
Habitat and Church Sts.
Americus, GA 31709-6935

Children and Youth at Risk Project
2233 Wisconsin Avenue, NW, Suite 215
Washington D.C. 20007
(202) 338-1831

Children's Defense Fund
25 E Street, NW
Washington, D.C. 20001
(202) 628-8787

National Law Center on Homelessness and Poverty
918 F Street, NW, Suite 412

Washington, D.C. 20004
(202) 638-2535

YMCA of the USA
101 North Wacker Drive
Chicago, IL 60606
(312) 977-0031

YWCA of the USA
726 Broadway
New York, NY 10003
(212) 614-2700

Canadian Resources

Canadian Red Cross Society
1800 Alta Vista Drive
Ottawa, ON K1G 4J5
(613) 739-3000

Family and Community Support Services Association of Alberta
4732-91 Avenue, 2nd Floor
Edmonton, AB T6B 2L1

Family Service Association of Metropolitan Toronto
22 Wellesley Street E
Toronto, ON M4Y 1G3

Alcohol and Drug Dependency Information and Counseling
Services (ADDICS)
#2, 2471 1/2 Portage Avenue
Winnipeg, MB R3J 0N6
(204) 831-1999

Alcoholics Anonymous
#502, Intergroup Office
234 Enlington Avenue E.
Toronto, ON M4P 1K5
(416) 487-5591

For Further Reading

Atkin, S. Beth, *Voices from the Street*. Boston: Little Brown and Co., 1996.

Berck, Judith, *No Place to Be*. Boston: Houghton Mifflin Co., 1992.

Johnson, Joan J., *Kids Without Homes*. New York: Franklin Watts, 1991.

Kenyon, Thomas L., with Blau, Justine, *What You Can Do to Help the Homeless*. New York: Simon & Schuster, 1991.

Kurland, Morton L., *Coping with Family Violence*, rev. ed. New York: The Rosen Publishing Group, 1990.

Kroloff, Rabbi Charles A., *54 Ways You Can Help the Homeless*. New Jersey: Hugh Lauter Levin Assoc, Inc., and Behrman House, Inc., 1993.

Landau, Elaine, *The Homeless*. New York: Simon & Schuster, Inc., 1987.

O'Connor, *Homeless Children*. San Diego: Lucent Books, 1989.

Index